Montessori First-ti:

First-Time Mom? You Need the Modern Toddler Approach with Disciplines Using Easy Baby-Led Weaning, No-Cry Baby, Deep Sleep and Potty Trainings for Your Kids (Age 0-6)

By

CHRISTY WISE

Table of Contents

Introduction

Infants are born incomplete at conception. It is our given role as adults to help our children in the formidable task of nesting their own human formation. Only in this manner, our children will become fully trained adults and achieve the ability they are able to attain from birth. For both the adult human and his human child, the degree of this challenge sets humans apart from all other species. However, their task is pre-programmed largely by their genes, and their instincts follow a narrowly limited developmental path. Given the care required for their species by the plan of creation, they need only time to grow larger and mature into adulthood. They pay the price though for their existence's predetermined nature. Their adaptation to their environment has limited versatility. Foal and calf, for example, are destined for eating grasses and grains; tiger and lion cub, small mammals. The ways they face certain challenges of life are also programmed: their fur keeps them dry, they are protected by horns and sharp teeth, swift legs take them from danger, and so forth.

On the other hand, the human child is born with no set pattern of instinctive behavior to satisfy its basic survival needs; its options are limitless. No predetermined response limits our ability to identify ways to meet our core food, shelter, clothing, transportation, and defense needs. We are given propensities to certain actions rather than the specific instructions of instincts. Though we are born naked and defenseless without a means of shelter and without instinctual knowledge of what is safe and right for us to eat, we have more than survived through these propensities; our behavioral tendencies account for the development and growth of all the varied civilizations from prehistoric people to the modern era of telecommunications throughout the ages; To help us appreciate how children react to the world in which they are raised, Montessori offered a summary of these propensities. She has no intention of restricting or actually refusing any set of behaviors. No doubt anyone of us will come up with our own different list.

In comparison to conventional teacher-centric teaching, Montessori teaching focuses on empowering kids to guide their own thinking. Teachers direct and give guidance to the students while allowing students to select their assignments and determine how to tackle each difficulty better. Children entering Montessori schools are learning to respect teamwork, keeping inside the guidelines, and worrying about how their behaviors affects others. Students maintain their imagination because of their enjoyment of learning and their own innate interest and drive themselves to succeed. Montessori children are taught how to incorporate a more comprehensive perspective into their knowledge over and above traditional school topics and are motivated to be interested and imaginative pupils. This book will act as a complete guide for you if you are new to the Montessori approach and have difficulty deciding whether to send your child to a Montessori school.

Chapter 1: Introduction to the Montessori Approach

When researching your child's Montessori schooling, it is important to learn a little about Montessori is past and how the approach came to be. Established approximately ten centuries ago, the Montessori Approach was the result of years of work undertaken by Dr. Maria Montessori, the renowned Italian psychiatrist, innovator, and educationist.

1.1 The History of Montessori

The Montessori education approach aims at the best potential growth of the child, training him ideally for the many rich encounters of life. Complemented by her scientific, developmental, and anthropological experience, Dr. Maria Montessori (1870 – 1952) formulated her teaching theory based on the empirical experiences of children.

Who was Maria Montessori?

Maria Montessori is often called 'before her time.' She is best regarded as the initiator of this famous method known as Montessori today. She was a woman wise beyond her years, determined and unwavering toward the conventions of society.

Born to her parents in Italy in 1870, Maria Montessori later moved to Rome with her parents in her early years, at the age of five in 1875. Maria was determined and curious for learning as a young child, and her mother encouraged her to achieve her academic endeavors, despite the fact that her father did not want her to continue education after her secondary school. While her father Alessandro supported conventional views of education for women, it was her mother's more radical approach, Renilde Montessori that inspired Maria Montessori to pursue her natural ability to know, irrespective of the social constraints imposed on women in today's men-dominated society. By doing so, Renilde took an important part in the education of her daughter, and thus, the whole theory of what is commonly regarded as the "Montessori Approach." At age 13, Montessori attended a vocational school for all-boys in order to pursue engineering. She continued following technical school to pursue her vision of becoming an engineer. She then entered La Sapienza High School at the University of Rome, earning a degree in medicine. Montessori's toughest struggle in medical college was constantly belittled by her colleagues in a male-dominated profession and required to study cadavers by themselves at night (because of university rules). Montessori stay consisted and eventually became Italy's first female scientist. She would be working in different areas that shaped her future: psychiatry wards and pediatrics clinics (one for kids) hospitals.

After Montessori graduated from the Rome University, she worked in the clinical department of the institution, also accompanying children in Rome's insane general asylums. During such experiences, she became persuaded that even such babies, deemed "mentally defective" and ignored by the normas, could be taught. During her period, her involvement in children's growth developed – first from her encounter with autistic children and the deplorable condition of their welfare at the period, then with mentally ill children in her welfare. When she benefited from the research of those already achieved in the area of early childhood education, she developed her own hypotheses, incorporating concepts, insights, and approaches in all fields, and she had studied.

Maria Montessori then created the foremost Casa Dei Bambini, or "Children's Home," in 1906, at the age of 36, for working-class children of the industrial revolution in one of the worst slum districts in town. With some 60 kids in her charge, Maria Montessori launched their education by teaching the older kids how to help with everyday chores. Knowing tools she had already created was added, and Montessori learned, to her delight, how small children instinctively adjusted and loved doing daily activities. The job environment and positive interaction brought the kids a sense of self-worth, which they had never felt before.

One of the first big obstacles Dr. Montessori encountered in changing these children's life was done by convincing parents to realize that their kids were unique and of tremendous importance. The Montessori Approach evolved from this respect for human appearance and potentiality. Via her findings, they established crucial stages in early childhood growth, and the approach developed to tackle these phases through age-appropriate learning materials and activities. Further advancement of the approach followed what Montessori defined as "cosmic schooling" – where the atmosphere and direction for children will be provided to become the peacekeepers of the future, residing in equilibrium with all living things in a prosperous universe.

The common philosophy of the day was that infants were "clean slates" and willing to learn from a parent or older child by clear guidance. In comparison, Montessori claimed that children had an inherent ability for learning and exploring — and were, in reality, motivated to do so. The educator's job, then, was to cultivate this inner ability, examine each child carefully, and provide him or her with activities that would enable him or her to learn the information and skills necessary for their developmental stage. Montessori said they do not need to be pushed to know when children are presented with appropriate resources in a safe, organized environment; yes, they are willing to learn.

In tumultuous times, Maria Montessori followed her values. Living through conflict and international instability encouraged her to complement the Montessori program with peace education. Yet she could do nothing to stop becoming involved in incidents across the globe. Traveling to India in 1940, she was forced to remain in exile for the duration of the war after wars broke out between Italy and Great Britain. She used the chance of her system to educate teachers there.

Maria Montessori expanded her research from this period until her death in 1952 and was generally known and accepted in the United States, Europe, and Asia. She has taught and established training sessions on these continents, set up a research institute in Spain and built training centers for Montessori in the Netherlands and London. Maria has advocated actively, as a public official, on behalf of women's rights. She often wrote and talked on the need for greater equality for women, and was known as a prominent feminist voice in Italy and beyond.

She returned to Europe towards the conclusion of the war and lived her final years in Amsterdam. She died peacefully, on May 6, 1952, in a friend's backyard. Maria Montessori had been a three-time Nobel Peace Laureate winner – in 1949, 1950, and 1951. The campaign she had established in 1907 had dropped out of favor at the time and in the United States was practically non-existent. The Montessori system, however, encountered a resurgence in the US after Dr. Nancy McCormick Rambusch, an early childhood education pioneer, started campaigning for it. She managed to open two Montessori schools, helped establish the American Montessori Society and published a book named: Learning How to Learn: An American Montessori Approach.

How the Montessori Method Evolved

During the year 1896, Montessori gave a speech on her observations from dealing with these special kids at the Educational Congress in Torino. The Education minister was interested and fascinated by the observations of Montessori named her as the head of an organization called Scuola Ortofrenica which was mainly made for the treatment and academics of the developmentally disabled. Montessori called her professional teaching, studying the girls, evaluating ideas, and constructing supplies for her two years there. She concluded, "I think there was nothing peculiarly restrictive about the techniques that I used to teach fools about them. I assumed that the ideals of education were more logical than in practice, much more, indeed, that an inferior mindset might evolve and thrive through its means. This thought, as profound in the form of an emotion, was my guiding concept after I was no longer in my school for shortcomings and, gradually, I was persuaded that identical approaches adapted to regular children would improve or activate their personalities in a marvelous and unexpected fashion." -The Montessori Way, Maria Montessori

Montessori noticed that and felt that if such approaches took children with intellectual disorders to the stage of regular children, after which she understood if that would improve typical children's ability. She got her opportunity to investigate that early. Only a short period after this finding was public, Montessori was approached to open a school which was located in a Rome housing estate. The children played easily and, when their guardians were at work because they were sometimes abusive. The planners used Montessori as a way to rein down the poor children and preserve their residential scheme.

In January 1907, the school in San Lorenzo began and was known as Casa dei Bambini, as well as Children's Home. Montessori provided the children and chance to think about puzzles as well as more, other fascinating meaningful things by teaching them daily tasks. The time Montessori stayed in Casa dei Bambini added in helping her to learn and refine her system further.

Montessori developed a natural world for the children, a world in which "there are no barriers to a their progress, they are eliminated and everything fits his or her age and maturity, and where he or she is allowed means to practice his developing ability" (Lillard and Montessori: A New Method, n. 4).

Montessori's philosophy stated that learning can no longer only express information, but rather follow a different direction, trying to unleash individual potentialities. Montessori was shocked by how pleased and fulfilled the children were as they worked on a subject of importance, often repeating it. Children learnt to do it themselves, to fix their faults and mistakes, to have the right to choose their jobs and resources, and not to seek a praise or penalty for their actions. She found the students were not much concerned about rewards, and often even did not pay attention to the prize or distributed it to someone else if they were rewarded. She claimed that the children wanted a feeling of human integrity and felt it in the workplace.

She has observed that children enjoy discipline, ethical awareness, real-life jobs using actual resources, peaceful jobs, and socially appropriate personal treatment. She admired the person and trusted in his potential. As the reports of the school's performance spread around, more people became increasingly involved in Montessori and her system. Therefore, Montessori began offering seminars, publishing pamphlets and subsequently books, additionally even teacher training in the process. Montessori sought to innovate in her theory, to explore the desires and talents of children and to build an atmosphere and resources that will bring in the maximum ability of the infant.

Montessori travelled widely across countries like the India and from Europe to America in her later years, offering classes, conducting training and workshop courses, going to different colleges, and exhibiting her classrooms at exhibits. She has won numerous awards, and has been nominated three times for the famous Nobel Peace Prize. She has also won various awards and titles in all of Europe. She conducted her last and final teacher-training session in the year before her death and presented at the International Council of Montessori (IMC), lived during two wars several of her sessions centered on teaching children to grow in harmony. Montessori showed the society a modern way of raising girls, a form in which schooling offered life and exploration.

Montessori & Educational Theory

Situating Montessori in Montessori's Educational Philosophy analysis of mental disorders in children inspired her to research education as a far more general field. She agreed that in curriculum foundations, she wanted to seek research that is more specialized. She headed to the University of Rome, where she studied psychology, sociology, history of education and theory, and concepts of pedagogy.

At the start of the twentieth century, the field of educational philosophy that Montessori joined was itself experiencing radical reconstruction. Although textbooks and recitations often controlled school teaching, intellectual thinkers like Rousseau, Pestalozzi, and Froebel had offered fresh insights into the essence of childhood and the schooling of girls.

Throughout his seminal work, Emile, the French philosopher Rousseau expounded a philosophy of natural education under which children were liberated from restrictive societal conventions. Notwithstanding Rousseau's insistence on the independence of children, Montessori considered much to be doubted in the theories of Rousseau, particularly his romantic belief that children learn better by pursuing their desires and urges in an unstructured natural world. Swiss educator Johann Heinrich Pestalozzi (1774–1827) established an instructional philosophy that encouraged classrooms to be turned into homely environments where children feel socially comfortable and learned with the use of their senses through specially crafted interactive lessons. Pestalozzi's focus on learning by experience and engaging with objects was a precursor in Montessori's emphatic practice. Of the three educators, Montessori was more frequently associated and contrasted with the kindergarten author, the German educator Friedrich Froebel (1782–1852).

Like Montessori, Froebel had introduced the notion that early childhood education would take place in a specially designed environment, kindergarten, or "child's garden." According to Froebel, a follower of idealistic theory, children were born with inner divine forces that flourished in an educational setting that promoted learning through self-activity and the unique use of perfect tools. By advocating the integrity and equality of children, she noticed that Rousseau, Pestalozzi, and Froebel had focused on a spiritual understanding of youth rather than an empirical one. They had deduced what it is like to be an infant by introspecting their childhood memories and had extended these beliefs to include all of childhood. Wild romanticism by Rousseau had overlooked the need for a formal learning atmosphere for the boy. The focus Pestalozzi put on utilizing objects as the foundation for learning was too rigid, repetitive, and automatic, though on the right track. Froebel's nursery was so steeped in metaphysical idealism that it was not rooted in contemporary psychology and research. Although acknowledging the achievements of her contemporaries, Montessori will correct their deficiencies by shifting clinically for her theories on the instructional approach to the direct evaluation of children. Around the same period as Montessori had agreed to establish a science-oriented pedagogy in Italy, educators were gaining fresh ideas into schooling elsewhere in the world. In the U.S., innovative educators have been implementing modern teaching approaches.

While Dewey's theory was focused on relativism, Montessori concentrated on universals. The prominent radical William Heard Kilpatrick (1871–1965) became an early and staunch opponent of Montessori.

Kilpatrick adapted Dewey's analytical theory to his widely famous system of projecting. Kilpatrick would fault Montessori for being out-of-date and ineffective in the socializing and imagination areas of the kid. In early childhood education, these radical educators — Parker, Dewey, Kilpatrick — who would become influential forces in American educational philosophy were following a different direction than Montessori's. The socialists tended to emphasize the school as an emerging, socially responsible community in which children studied in a permissive setting utilizing the empirical method. The progressives, calling enthusiastically for democracy in education, denied the role of absolute principles and urged freedom and activity. Montessori's philosophy of schooling will vary from that of the American progressives, with its focus on studying in a formal setting using didactic content.

Even Europe has developed yet another significant way of looking at childhood. In Vienna, Sigmund Freud (1856–1939), through his formulation of psychoanalytic psychology, began to understand the role performed by the abnormal through human growth and development.31 Like Rousseau, Pestalozzi, and Froebel had proposed, youth, Freud realized, was more than accidental liberation and imitative play. It was more than an opportunity to become political actors in an open-ended culture, as advocated by Dewey, Kilpatrick, and the American progressives. Freud's theories have begun to reshape the creation of the existence of babies. To him, early childhood was a period of erotic desires and social deprivation that formed the mind of the human being and had implications for the identity of adults. The "Oedipus complex" was a Freud hypothesis established regarding infant anatomy, in which the child wished to own the opposite sex parent. Freud claimed children are moving through a series of phases of psychosexual development. When at some single period, the infant became over gratified or repressed, so at that point the attitude would become set. The way needs were fulfilled or prevented had implications for the self-esteem of the individual and financial, social, and sexual relationships. Lingering unresolved issues and disputes that arise throughout the developmental phases may trigger issues of internal health and transition during a person's existence. Psychoanalytical treatment was a process by which the problem was established, embedded in the subconscious, and brought to awareness. The individual may identify the problem in this way, analyze it and solve it.

There were several similarities in their career choices, which Freud and Montessori took. Like Montessori, Freud was a pediatric student who then went on to psychiatry, treating psychiatric disorders and specialized in neurology. Montessori and Freud also have come up with a philosophy on infant growth. Freud schooled in the United States, as did Montessori. Freud and Montessori were mindful of the opinions on early childhood within themselves. While both Montessori and Freud called for the liberation of infants, their creation philosophies were very different. Montessori dismissed Freud's views about child identity and the long-term importance of subsequent psychological, interpersonal conflict.32 A Biography and Review 13 Around 1904 and 1908; Montessori started to create her own position in the world of education. She lectured on the application of sociology and genetics to education at the University of Rome's Pedagogical Level.

Montessori's push into the world of physiological anthropology was part of a broader growth of science and social science of Italy at the time. In Italy, Cesare Lombroso and Giuseppe Sergi founded the area of physical anthropology. Montessori was acquainted with Lombroso's work on criminal anatomy, which included taking unlawful measures, in particular the size and form of the head and neck, and seeking to generalize the illegal sort to any conclusion. She was most inspired by Sergi, who created the University of Rome's Institute of Experimental Psychology, and with whom she worked. Physical anthropology reflects on the human being's biological research as a natural organism; it utilizes analytical methods to calculate, chart, and analyze individual anatomical and morphological differences. The subfield, anthropometry, tests the physical features of people using different instruments.

Montessori expanded schooling into the area of physiological anthropology. In particular, she emphasized the significance of taking accurate physical measurements of children's height, weight, head, pelvis, and limbs as well as identifying some sort of malformations. Such metrics were to be documented regularly as an individualized scientific database, a biographical map to be held for each boy. She focused her lectures on the topics of the empirical approach to pedagogy, the proper methods of scientifically studying both dysfunctional and average children, the science evidence collection and analysis techniques, and how this anthropological knowledge could be used to generalize instructional approaches.

Montessori, a renowned educator, established a reputation among the learners because of her strongly inspired and enthusiastic presentations. Because she was able to draw from a range of fields, from nursing to sociology to psychology, she offered her students an extraordinary multidisciplinary scope of knowledge at the time. Drawing from her history resources in nursing, neuroscience, and (their new interest) sociology. She presented her lectures as L'Antropolgia Pedagogica (Pedagogical Anthropology), a book that incorporates concepts from clinical science, infant psychology, and cultural anthropology and extended them to the growth and education of children. What was starting to arise at this point in Montessori's creation as an instructional thinker was a systematic philosophy of schooling derived from various academic areas. She demonstrated her habit of taking a holistic and multidisciplinary approach to teaching by drawing components from her background in medicine, psychology, and anthropology (their latest interest).

About Casa Die Bambini

The Casa Dei Bambini, a significant opportunity in the profession of Montessori, came in 1907 when Edoardo Talamo requested her to create a school in Rome's slum town. At the time, Talamo was managing director of the Istituto Romano di Beni Stabili (the Strong Building Association), a charitable organization founded to enhance poor people's housing conditions. The association bought and remodeled run-down, overcrowded, and unsanitary tenements in the area. It has been engaged in housing reconstruction in the quarter of San Lorenzo, a part of

15

Rome plagued by violence. The invitation Talamo made to Montessori was an effort to address a very realistic question. When parents who resided in redeveloped housing went to college, their children were left alone and unsupervised in kindergarten. For these babies, the association agreed to create the school as some kind of daycare center.

Nevertheless, Montessori has already had the ability to build a school that will act as a classroom for exploring her theories. John Dewey, too, was researching his theoretical theories at the University of Chicago Laboratory School is much more desirable conditions. In both educators' situations, such educational studies will create their identities as leading educators.

On January 6, 1907, Montessori founded her first kindergarten, the Casa Dei Bambini, or Children's Home, in a large property on Via Dei Marsi 58, in the poverty-ridden district of San Lorenzo, Rome. Her first pupils were fifty students, between the ages of three and seven, whose families resided in the house. The district of San Lorenzo, a deprived slum town, was similar to those found in Europe and America's growing big cities. Just like Montessori, on the west side of Chicago, Jane Addams, the influential American social worker, had designed a settlement house for the needy, Hull Home. The Casa Dei Bambini and the Hull House were but two of the attempts by philanthropic and educational means to relieve the suffering of the needy.

In post-Risorgimento Italy, internal migration brought to cities like Milan and Rome, in pursuit of jobs, large flowing waves of former peasants. Tenement districts emerged in these cities to accommodate the urban underclass. This subset in an urban environment was ill prepared for life. Montessori named the squalid conditions — crime and vice — they witnessed a dark "land of darkness" in the San Lorenzo district. Despite such modern solutions to urban schooling as the American "Project Head Start" for approximately one hundred years, Montessori recognized the critical significance that early childhood education provided for eventual progress. In the case of children impacted by poverty, they needed to receive the kind of knowledge, which could bring them out of the cycle of deprivation. She found the school to be the original microcosmic history and a 15th Study attempt at a greater endeavor to bring about societal change by way of schooling. Montessori's broad awareness of the essence of social progress and its connection to education put her among the early twentieth century's leading social reformers.

Montessori was driven in establishing the Casa Dei Bambini by the sociological and educational goals she had set throughout the different stages of her life. Located inside the tenement, in which the families of the children stayed, the school was to serve as a crucial organic bridge between schooling and community, embodied by the teachers. Not only was her approach a way of teaching children more humanely and efficiently, but it was meant to help the poor inhabitants of San Lorenzo recover socially. Unlike Jane Addams, Montessori argued that in contemporary life, like in the earlier traditional definition of welfare, help should no longer be in the way of providing alms to the needy.

In the past, assistance was provided to support the victims of deprivation and sickness through well-intentioned people. Montessori argued in the modern era, with its rapid urbanization and industrialization, that the idea of private charity had to be rethought and developed into a more systematic and oriented effort to bring about social reform. If more extensive, more organized, and expected efforts were made to eliminate poverty sectors such as San Lorenzo, Montessori worried that there would be a great divide in modern society, a wide chasm dividing rich and poor. Unless the pattern persisted, the disadvantaged would be trapped in poverty-ridden ghettoes, which Montessori named "islands of the oppressed." The principles of welfare had to be rebuilt in the new period not just to bring temporary relief to the needy, but also to alleviate the circumstances that induced social and economic deprivation. By establishing existing programs to deter sickness, enhance health and sanitation, inform children and adults, and transform culture, human welfare had to be socialized. Montessori believed that such government institutions will boost the standard of living, be more productive than unorganized community actions, promote economic growth, and render citizens autonomous of the dole.

The Children's House was built educationally to be a school-home, an educational entity in near proximity to the families of infants. In reality, it was in the house where the kids lived. Montessori said, "We brought the school inside the building.

The school would lead to the socialization of the family and the household, which would in effect, bind the household with the greater community. The real geographical proximity of the children's home to the school had a social aspect linked to Montessori's concept of the "modern woman" of the twentieth century. Casa Dei Bambini was situated in a region of the working class where the majority of mothers employed in the emerging factories of Italy. However, Montessori proposed that in the future, not only working-class women should be hired outside the home, but also more people of all social backgrounds should enter the workplace. The guiding force in bringing about this shift in women's employment was industrialization and technical progress. Schools, as educational bodies, had to recognize this technology-driven transition to cater for working mother children. Schools like the Casa Dei Bambini would encourage mothers to leave their children comfortably and "begin their research with a feeling of great relief and independence." Despite the change in working habits and places, Montessori suggested that mothers would still have a greater obligation for the physical and moral treatment of their children. The Casa Dei Bambini would assist them in serving these parental duties when finding work and leisure beyond their home.40 Montessori then had many reasons in mind while creating the Casa Dei Bambini, the precursor of all present Montessori schools: first, the social and economic motivations of social reform, in particular, the enhancement of the working class's condition; second, third, the social and economic motives of social change; The Casa Dei Bambini, however, was mainly a venue for the education of children; establishing a social utopia was not a concept, nor was it merely a hub for daycare of children for working mothers. It provided schooling, as the new school for the modern age, based on the principles of scientific pedagogy.

One of Montessori's key pedagogical ideals was that instruction with children in a disciplined and organized setting was best accomplished. She requested that any specific rules extend to children attending her school and their guardians. The children were supposed to come to school with clean bodies and clothing, no matter how dirty they were. They must have been given a white dress or apron. Believing schools were most successful when closely related to the families and homes of the students, parents were encouraged to be involved in and endorse the education of their children and attend regular conferences, called "parent-directress" meetings (to be discussed below).

Like John Dewey from the University of Chicago Experimental School, Montessori made sure that the practical structures, desks, seats, and apparatuses of the school were tailored to the needs of children rather than adults. She did not want to limit the freedom of expression of the children in the classroom and its furniture, as it did in traditional schools. Tables and chairs were designed to match the heights and weights of the students. Washstands were placed for smaller children to reach. Classrooms were filled with small cupboards where kids could quickly access didactic materials and be liable for taking them back to their proper location. The Montessori school was built to foster the sensory sensitivity and manual ability of children, give them a degree of option within a controlled atmosphere, create a climate of order, and improve independence and self-assurance in performing skills.

Montessori's understanding of the teacher's position differed from conventional schools. While teachers in traditional elementary schools dominated the middle of the instructional stage as the focal point for the interest of the students, Montessori called her instructor a "directress" who was to lead the students while they learned themselves to understand. The director, a properly trained instructor in the Montessori system, was to instruct the children in their own self-development.41 Skilled in children's health assessment and science pedagogy, the director was to be attentive to infant preparation and developmental phases. With its correct apparatus and resources, she was to develop the prepared atmosphere and cooperate in the self-education of the children.

1.2 Need of Montessori & Its Benefits

Before this chapter discusses the need of Montessori and why it was important for it to form, below is a brief introduction of what the Montessori is about.

From The American Montessori Society: The Montessori Philosophy of Schooling, founded by Dr. Maria Montessori, is an instructional methodology focusing on children from infancy to maturity focused on empirical findings. Dr. Montessori's Approach has been studied over decades, with more than 100 years of global popularity in different societies.

It is a perception of the individual as one who is instinctively excited about the information and willing to facilitate learning in a positive, thoughtfully planned learning environment. This is a philosophy that respects the human soul, and the entire child's development — physical, financial, mental, cognitive.

Montessori schooling provides resources for our children to grow their talents when they venture out into the world when dedicated, knowledgeable, conscientious, and compassionate people with awareness and reverence that learning is for life.

Any child is regarded as a unique adult. Montessori teaching acknowledges that children work in many contexts, and adapts to these forms of learning. Students are often able to study at their own rate, always moving when they are ready through the program, directed by the instructor, and an individualized learning plan. Montessori students start at an early age and build discipline, communication, focus, and freedom. Classroom architecture, facilities, and day-to-day activities help the evolving "self-regulation" of the person (capacity to teach one's self, and care about what one is learning), by adolescents. Students are part of a community that is close and caring. A family dynamic is re-created by the multi-age classroom — typically lasting three years. Older students value status as leaders and role models; newer pupils feel encouraged by the obstacles ahead and develop trust. Teachers are demonstrating empathy, love kindness, and a belief in the successful settlement of the dispute. Students of Montessori practice equality inside the limits. Operating under guidelines established by their professors, students are actively interested in determining what their learning emphasis should be. Montessorians believe that intrinsic happiness stimulates the imagination and excitement of the infant and results in happy, life-long learning that is lasting. Students are motivated to become successful aspirants of information. Teachers have areas in which students are granted the opportunity and opportunities to answer their own concerns.

Self-correction or self-assessment form an integral part of the Montessori approach to the classroom. When students mature, they continue to look objectively at their work and learn from their experiences and understand, evaluate, and improve. Montessori students are positive, active, self-directed learners with the freedom and encouragement to inquire, to explore deeply, and to create connections. They should think creatively, function collaboratively, and behave courageously — an ability set for the 21st century.

1.1   The Traditional Method vs. Montessori Method

Montessori is distinct from conventional education in areas relevant to the future Mainstream Curriculum promotes a one-size-fits-all method to instruction, which sees the infant as a blank canvas to compose on.

The instructor offers the learners information. Rote memorization of information is prevalent in many mainstream classrooms, where kids are sitting at a desk gleaning whatever info they can from the instructor standing at the front of the room. The classroom at Montessori is a "prepared atmosphere," which promotes individual development and learning. Kids will travel across the space to select from a wide variety of crafted materials placed on well-organized shelves. We develop practical and analytical skills by independently studying vocabulary, arithmetic, geography, astronomy, painting, music, and more. Parents new to Montessori's environment often remember how peaceful the classroom is, how great it sounds, and how centered the kids are. This is because they are focused on the learning "job."

So, among the first questions that pop up with many parents when selecting their children's nursery or daycare is whether they will go for one that follows the Montessori system or one that incorporates a play-based methodology. Here are some of the main differences — and what else you can think before you make your choice.

Maria Montessori dig upon the Montessori Theory of Education in the early 1900s. Montessori has a deep belief in human development. She created a modern approach to education focused on her study of children from diverse ethnic, religious, and socioeconomic backgrounds. It was fast expanding too many nations and continents. The First Montessori School in Canada began in 1912, and there are more than 500 in the world today.

Montessori schools believe play is the job of a child. Their services are geared at adolescents, promoting positive, self-paced, individualized learning. Children pick tasks for continuous periods, focused on their preferences and "jobs." Teachers monitor and chart their development, to allow their usage of resources simpler. Via this strategy, children are assumed to become more comfortable, more autonomous, more self-regulated, and more self-disciplined.

Whereas, play-centered traditional schools are focused on the idea that children learn better by practice. Although the playtime is open-ended and unfocused, these pre-schools can be more teacher-directed. Children engage in a broad range of activity-based events, including pretending to play, and teachers respond with learning lessons. In fact, children are improving their problem-solving, teamwork, dispute management, and social skills.

Both Montessori and play-based pre-schools should provide cultures that are inclusive and carefully planned. Usually, Montessori pre-schools are split into five learning areas: English, arithmetic, daily life, sensory, and cultural. Play-oriented centers may often be grouped into events or themes centered areas or stations.

Carol Anne Wien, a retired Montessori instructor and professor emeritus from the School of Education at York University in Toronto, states a significant institutional difference: "Modern school settings seem to be strongly time-oriented — whether you realize what time it's, you realize what the kids are doing — but it's poorly spatially oriented. Montessori is the reverse: very spatially organized and poorly defined in time. When you know where the kids are in the house, you know what they are doing, so it is free time. Teachers prefer to switch between making the kids play and performing instructional exercises in play-based childcare. "Montessori settings appear to be simpler, calmer, and less intense than activity-based settings, which some kids might consider too noisy, bright, or high-stimulus, Wien says. She says, "Look for a peaceful atmosphere, one in which the color comes from the kids and their games and drawings, no matter what sort of pre-school you want. Be very vigilant of an atmosphere overflowing with red, yellow and blue, and big, heavy amounts of print or animated figures, and so on, as they are very physically disturbing for the infant and can wear the infant out.

The Advantages

A major advantage for Montessori is that the child is engaged at his own speed and time, "says Wien, adding the children can are overwhelmed in a convention." Kids often appear to become strongly self-regulated in Montessori systems. That's a major benefit, as it's called, at this point, a huge requirement for school success — not intellect but the capacity to self-regulate. "(Self-regulation implies how easily an individual returns to a stable state after experiencing stress.)

In play-based environments, Wien says, children's imaginations can really thrive, and so their social skills can thrive, such as creating friendships and working through things. "These are both all good stuff. I might suggest that Montessori had little likelihood of tolerating abstract or creative activity. In a play-based child care facility, which is also a successful path to self-regulation, you can have more socio-dramatic activity. "The temperament and attitude of your child will affect your choice. Some kids do best at one or the other environment. "When you have a really busy little boy who likes to play aircraft and create with bricks, I will place him in a play-based system," Wien says. "When you have a timid kid that holds back, and you're not sure what they're involved in, I'd place them in a Montessori system where they have this warm, warm setting that will bring them out in ways you haven't seen before." Making the decision Note, both Montessori and play centers help children train for kindergarten and cultivate a love of learning, so they both have to stick with the laws. All ideologies may also deliver excellent systems and poor ones — you cannot judge only by theory.

In reality, Wien would not prescribe that parents automatically chose between nursery or daycare based on play and Montessori. "The key criteria is to go to the core to search for the consistency of the relationships between educators to adolescents, the educators and each other, and the parents, of course," she says. "It is going to inform the parent whether they choose to put their child in the system."

Differences between Montessori and Pre-school

It is a huge choice to determine the right way to take your kid to nursery or kindergarten. When you want to determine where he or she is most likely to succeed, there are one million things to weigh. Education choices and styles vary in certain places, rendering the choice more complicated, in several respects. A Montessori School is one way out there. However, how precisely is a school like a

Montessori renowned for its radical practices separate from a conventional kindergarten or pre-school? Below are some of the key variations.

Mixed-age classroom

In a conventional kindergarten, by a certain cutoff date (typically September 1), each infant in the classroom should have had his or her fifth birthday, which ensures that at the beginning of the year every kid in the classroom should be 5, with some turning six throughout the school year.

Montessori colleges also, though, have mixed generation classes. A school for kindergartens involves children aged 3-6. She is the Fountainhead Montessori School Coordinator in Dublin, California. She has worked with Montessori for six years and takes her children to a Montessori school. According to her, one advantage of the mixed-age classroom is that it offers an opportunity for older children to be members. "On a regular basis, I see older students saying 'stand back and wait' to younger students and the older student talking to the younger student." Besides the trust that this would certainly offer the older pupil, it is also a means of showing knowledge of the material and ensuring it has been maintained. The younger child is confident hearing from someone they can respond easily to.

Individualization

Individualized schooling is today one of the buzzwords of the curriculum. About every education-from the most conservative to the most modern-claims to deliver individualized instruction, but it does not often happen in reality. In addition, individualization differs in degree.

However, Montessori schools are built on, and stick to, a belief in individualization in education. All is handled at the speed of the infant with the idea that any kid on his or her own period reaches milestones. "We are bringing a kid as he/she is at present and having them navigate a growth path," says her. "They develop their abilities at their own rate." In a place of their choosing, even a child will understand. "You should sit at the desk here, lie on a mat, or walk about the classroom easily," She says. "There are resources accessible to support children to discover what makes them feel relaxed."

Hands-On

There would be hands-on exercises in a typical nursery or kindergarten classroom because educators understand the desire to include children. Yet as to the degree to which hands-on instruction is used, Montessori varies from conventional schooling. According to her, "Everything is really real and hands-on in a Montessori [classroom]." There is the intention to include as many senses as possible in learning. The hands-on learning in a pre-school or kindergarten in Montessori may look more like playing and or having fun to the kid, but it is purposive.

Therefore, Which One is Right for Your Child

Although she says that every child with a Montessori capacity will succeed, she refers to inspiration as providing a boost to the students. "The students who are performing especially well are inspired emotionally," she says.

Certain characteristics also improve the likelihood of a pupil at a Montessori school to excel. Children of a Montessori school would want to cooperate, socialize, and work on their own continue to perform well. When it comes to kindergarten students, standards about these kinds of items are fewer. "Younger students at our school are also forming the characteristics that will benefit them, and they get more support than those at the upper grades," She says. "At the end of the day, the Montessori curriculum is intended to function best for all children because it is child-friendly." The Bottom Line While a Montessori school is distinct from a conventional system; certain common concepts do apply. Those involve a passion for studying, the inculcation of knowledge to help children excel, and moral accountability. The expectations revolve around four characteristics at a Montessori school: discipline, focus, teamwork, and freedom. "When such characteristics can be inculcated by children, they will adapt them to everything that they do and be effective," says her.

Understanding that there are several choices when you decide what sort of school to send your child too. You will find a system with persistence and dedication that will encourage your kid to achieve his / her ability.

How to Choose Between Montessori and Preschool:

If you have all the details before you, the problem then is, what pre-school is right for your child? Although many parents assume that school is a one-size fit all incentives, the fact is that each child has various talents, various shortcomings and all should value specific forms of learning that. Montessori's similarities over conventional education are numerous. However, in educational theory alone, the option, which is right for a single child, does not always lie. Ask yourself these questions while trying to distinguish between a conventional pre-school classroom and a Montessori classroom:

1. What Was The Purpose Of My Sending To Pre-School?

The target for some parents is to find childcare, which also requires necessary social and academic skills such as counting, colors, and sharing. It is a feature in other typical classes at the nursery. Pre-school is an opportunity for other parents to recognize and develop a passion for learning and adventure that can take them into their academic years. Such guardians, in other terms, perceive the nursery as the gateway to years of academic achievement. That is where childhood Montessori fits in.

2. What kind of environment will benefit my child?

Modern classrooms in the nursery are also noted for vivid colors, lights, and the hustle and bustle of large children's groups at play. Colors become more subdued in a Montessori classroom, and natural light provides the children with the "hot" feeling when they know. Children's play is their "job" in both instances, although the conventional pre-school stresses imaginative play as a way of learning and development. At the same time, Montessori encourages creative tasks that are often intellectual, such as blocks of the wooden alphabet or learning to tie a shoe.

3. Who I Have My Child Attend Before Preschool Of School?

The Montessori approach of education is structured for the expectation that children should arrive at age 3 — or perhaps earlier — and then develop through many years through the curriculum. While certain schools may welcome older children, Montessori schools usually avoid enrolling high school-age children in their systems because they did not first take part in a pre-school Montessori curriculum. This is because it is harder for younger learners who have no previous learning encounters to adjust to the Montessori way of doing stuff.

On the other side, a conventional pre-school classroom is arranged to mimic the typical classes that would be met by children during their college life, irrespective of the school they attend. A traditional nursery, unlike Montessori, is not suitable for educating children before they enter primary school.

4. What Does My Child Need?

The last question welcomes the views and opinions on the three previous issues. There are benefits and drawbacks to all styles of services that it boils down to the kids. All certified, credible pre-school services share the aim of developing your child, training her for kindergarten, and fostering a love of learning. They are governed by the government of the State and responsible for the requirements it establishes.

Every kid has multiple talents, specific difficulties, and different learning styles. What encourages and encourages one child may annoy or shame another child. Although the mainstream curriculum is built with a one-size-fits-all mindset, no one-size-fits-all child exists. Stop and look around when you are trying to decide between Montessori or the traditional pre-school. Where do you want your child to thrive? And what would be of more value to them as they grow? The response to that query is, in the end, everything you need.

Montessori Teachers

One of the most noticeable distinctions between Montessori teachers and conventional teachers is the tremendous trust Montessori teachers put in the children's cognitive ability. To "follow the kid" requires an enormous amount of confidence. It is so much better to tell the kids, follow where I am going so that no one gets lost. Nonetheless, with close monitoring and preparation, Montessori instructors are continuously alert to growing child's progress and are working diligently to help them excel.

Teachers at Montessori are not the object of concern in the classroom. Their job centers on planning and arranging learning resources to match the Montessori children's needs and interests. The emphasis is on educating students, not training teachers.

As a mentor and facilitator, the Montessori instructor develops a well-prepared Montessori setting and an environment of learning and inquisitiveness intended to shift pupils from one experience and stage to the next. An instructor from Montessori also stands back as the kids work, encouraging them to benefit from their own experiences and come to their conclusions. Instead of presenting solutions to students, the Montessori instructor tells them if they can fix the issue, effectively engage students in the learning process, and develop clear thinking skills. For certain situations, rather than the tutor, children learn primarily from the environment, often from other youngsters.

Dr. Montessori claimed the instructor would concentrate on the infant as an individual rather than on the preparations for the everyday classes. While for each child, the Montessori instructor schedules regular lessons, she must be alert to shifts in the child's motivation, development, attitude, and actions.

The topics are interwoven, and the instructor of Montessori must be simple to explain and appreciate the works of literature, poetry, music, education, astronomy, zoology, botany, chemistry, physical geography, writing, physics, geometry, and physical existence. The tutor at Montessori is qualified to give one-on-one or small community lessons and to spend less time delivering big group lessons. The lectures are short and precise, designed to inspire children's minds such that they can come back and know all about themselves. Montessori lectures rely on the most critical knowledge, which the children need to perform the work:

- the name of the products
- where they can be placed in the classroom and on the table
- how to use the items
- In addition, what to do with them.

Teachers at Montessori become kid technology observers. They do not use bonuses and penalties for positive or weak jobs. Teachers at Montessori never criticize or intervene with the education of a pupil. It is only in a comfortable environment that the personality of a child has space to develop. Children must have the right to select their hobbies and experience unlimited conduct. Dr. Montessori assumed that this was a specific task and that the kid should show his / her true self after he/she had found a position demanding complete focus. In The Absorbent Mind (pp. 277-81), Maria Montessori, in the Montessori classroom, gave several basic standards of behavior to students. The teacher is an atmosphere keeper and custodian. She attends to that rather than being disturbed by the restlessness of the babies. All the equipment is carefully kept in place, in good shape, elegant and polished. This means the instructor must always be orderly and safe, calm, and dignified. Thus, the first responsibility of the instructor is to look over the community, so this takes priority over the others. Its impact is indirect, so there can be no successful and lasting consequences of any sort, physical, mental, or spiritual unless it is performed correctly.

In A Way of Learning (1973), Anne Burke Neubert identified the following elements in the Montessori teacher's specific role:

- Montessori teachers are the relational connection between the children and the Prepared Environment.

- They track their students regularly and perceive their needs.

- They continually explore, change the atmosphere to fulfill their expectations of the needs and desires of each child, and critically mention the outcome.

- They plan an atmosphere intended to promote the individuality of children and the freedom to openly choose work we consider appealing, select tasks that would cater to their preferences and maintain the setting in good shape, attach to it and withdraw materials when appropriate.

- Every day, they systematically examine the quality of their research and environmental architecture.

- They track and appraise the individual development of a growing boy.

- They admire the freedom of their pupils and defend it. They need to learn when to reach in to impose boundaries or offer a helping hand, and when it is in the better interest of a child to stand back and not intervene.

- They are welcoming, giving increasing child comfort, protection, security, and non-judgmental acceptance.

- They promote children's contact and help children understand how to express their feelings to adults.

- For parents, school workers, and the neighborhood, they view the success of the children and their performance in the classroom. They provide the children with straightforward, engaging, and valuable lessons. They seek to stimulate the child's curiosity and concentrate on environmental lessons and practices.

- They model positive behavior for the students, observing the class's ground rules, demonstrating a sense of calmness, integrity, dignity, and courtesy and displaying consideration for each child.

- They are the educators of harmony, working diligently to teach courteous attitudes and confrontation.

- They are diagnostic practitioners who can categorize patterns of growth, development, and behavior to better understand the children and make required referrals and suggestions for parents.

Have Trust

Montessori teachers recognize that parents will be "in the know" without needing to be at the forefront through diligent study and properly planned settings.

One of Montessori's most significant contrasts with conventional teachers is the direction the instructor perceives the infant. You may have learned that Montessori instructors "ignore the kid." Yet what you do not know is the degree of confidence (in the infant) it takes to step in and allow the child to truly take the lead. With youngsters, it is the normal tendency of the individual to assume a leadership position. Like little ducklings following our guide, we want to hold children in line securely. This way, we learn (or think we know) where everyone is and what they do. Yet Montessori instructors recognize that adults will stay "in the know," without needing to be at the forefront, through diligent attention and an adequately planned setting.

Teachers at Montessori are not the subject of the classroom. The emphasis is then on the kid getting the best experiences and resources to improve his or her learning. It is known and acknowledged in a Montessori classroom that a child will and should relax and focus until he seeks the correct "job." As Montessori put it, "the instructor will assume that this child can demonstrate his true nature to her when he discovers a piece of work that interests him. In addition, what would she have to watch out for? "This is the inventor's or discoverer's work, the explorer's valiant actions" This is not to imply that the Montessori instructor does not play an essential role in the education of the child. On the opposite, the position of the teacher as a guide is essential. I think of the instructor of Montessori as a Sherpa, a mentor whose indispensable help helps every little adventurer to achieve his unique zenith.

"But when work is the product of an inherent inner emotion; it takes a different form. Such research is exciting, addictive, and elevates man beyond deviations and contradictions inside. This is the inventor or discoverer's job, the explorer's valiant actions, or the artist's creations, that is, the work of people born with such remarkable strength that they may rediscover the characteristics of their race in the forms of their own uniqueness. ~D. Maria Montessori: The Childhood Code.

The Montessori instructor plans the environment (i.e., the classroom) based on each child's diligent and consistent observations. Therefore, the classroom offers learning resources that involve the infant in a developmentally acceptable way. The instructor can step back, enabling them to learn at their own speed, while the children are engaged in their activity of choice. At this level, the instructor does not need to have inspiration. The children are motivated by a desire to learn inside themselves.

"And then we learned that teaching is not something that the instructor does but a normal phenomenon that naturally occurs in the human person. This is not learned by listening to phrases, but by interactions through which the infant acts on his or her surroundings. The responsibility of the teacher is not to speak, but to plan and organize a set of reasons for cultural interaction in a specific atmosphere that is designed for the infant. "~ Dr. Maria Montessori, The Absorbent Mind

The first step is so frail, so delicate that contact will cause it to vanish again, like a soap bubble, and with it, all goes the Teachers from small group lessons as they pass across the classroom, and not just one lesson in front of the whole class. Lessons are realistic, simple, and designed to engage the child in order to pursue the exploration on its own. The Montessori instructor stands back after the child is engaged, and refrains from criticizing, complimenting, or even intervening in any way.

1.3 Montessori Education Today

It's been about 100 years that Dr. Maria Montessori began interacting with kids, but the research and impact of her career has changed our view of the kids and how they interact with the environment around them. Today, licensed Montessori schools around the globe are following the mission of Dr. Montessori, filled by Montessori-certified educators named 'guides' They strive to serve the entire child, helping children become competent, confident, interactive learners at all stages of growth. About a century later, the experience and ideology of her life help us appreciate how children are the secret to a more tranquil planet.

Luckily the Montessori process has survived over time, also included in numerous colleges. This supports games and children's freedom and individuality, as well as engagement to awaken fascination with varied components. In brief, it reaps the innate tendency of children for games and enjoyment, rendering it the key instructional motor.

However, the panorama shifts as we immerse ourselves in modern primary education. Kids spend hours paying proper attention to their instructors, getting disciplined for not communicating (or being criticized for doing so), being reluctant to talk, and trying to be vigilant for lengthy stretches. One class comes ahead of another. This specializes in stripping away all underlying learning incentives.

Several schools have opted for the Montessori system. Given all that, there is always some uncertainty. Is the Montessori approach not accessible to children aged between 0 and 6? While several schools still provide this approach even to this age range, the reality is that it was developed by Maria Montessori so that it could be implemented before she was 12 years old. Also, implement the Montessori approach can, however, at a high school level. Maria Montessori did leave some proven guidelines for the steps to be followed with older children, although she did not have time to plan and refine it entirely for this level. The existing method of schooling depends a lot on the classes. Therefore, a lot of responsibility is exerted on students to accomplish assignments that would contribute to a desirable final score. The reverse is what the Montessori approach wants. There are no tests and no assignments since the key aim is to know and not get the highest score. The evidence shows us that the schooling following primary school unsettles the pupils. Far from making them excited, it lets them realize that going to school is pointless. This condition will have an opportunity to rethink the way we teach. Competitiveness is nurtured today. Students of degrees mark as incompetent or wise. The primary aim, however, is to make students feel inspired to learn the environment around them.

Chapter 2: Understanding Montessori Curriculum for Raising Responsible & Curious Toddlers

The Montessori Philosophy of Schooling, founded by Dr. Maria Montessori, is an instructional methodology focusing on children from infancy to maturity focused on empirical findings. Dr. Montessori's Approach has been studied over decades, with more than 100 years of global popularity in different societies.

It is a perception of the individual as one who is instinctively excited about the information and willing to facilitate learning in a positive, thoughtfully planned learning environment. This is a philosophy that respects the human soul, and the entire child's development — physical, financial, mental, cognitive. Montessori schooling provides resources for our children to grow their talents when they venture out into the world when dedicated, knowledgeable, conscientious, and compassionate people with awareness and reverence that learning is for life.

2.1 The Montessori Curriculum

Every child is regarded as a unique adult. Montessori teaching acknowledges that children work in many contexts, and adapts to these forms of learning. Students are often able to study at their rate, always moving when they are ready through the program, directed by the instructor, and an individualized learning plan. Montessori students start at an early age and build discipline, communication, focus, and freedom. Classroom architecture, facilities, and day-to-day activities help the evolving "self-regulation" of the person (capacity to teach one's self, and care about what one is learning), by adolescents.

Students are part of a community that is close and caring. A family dynamic is re-created by the multi-age classroom — typically lasting three years. Older students value status as leaders and role models; newer pupils feel encouraged by the obstacles ahead and develop trust. Teachers are demonstrating empathy, love kindness, and a belief in the successful settlement of the dispute.

Students of Montessori practice equality inside the limits. Operating under guidelines established by their professors, students are actively interested in determining what their learning emphasis should be. Montessorians believe that intrinsic happiness stimulates the imagination and excitement of the infant and results in happy, life-long learning that is lasting. Students are motivated to become successful aspirants of information. Teachers have areas in which students are granted the opportunity and opportunities to answer their own concerns.

Self-correction or self-assessment form an integral part of the Montessori approach to the classroom. When students mature, they continue to look objectively at their work and learn from their experiences and understand, evaluate, and improve. Montessori students are positive, active, self-directed learners with the freedom and encouragement to inquire, to explore deeply, and to create connections. They should think creatively, function collaboratively, and behave courageously — an ability set for the 21st century.

Montessori Philosophy: Put Children First

On the theory of Montessori, they are not simply little people. They are young, and they deserve consideration in their own way and for whom they belong. This indicates, among other aspects, that they will be given the ability to read and gain trust in doing so, in developmentally acceptable ways. Maria Montessori has conducted hundreds of children's work. This ignited some observations in the way they trained. And, over time, it prompted her to believe that children would be put at the education center.

Since conception to age six, the Curriculum Children develop the foundation and identity they will have for the remainder of their lives. Because in this growth, creativity and fantasy play key roles, children require actual, factual facts to construct the framework and character with. Of that purpose, the program of Fountainhead Montessori is focused on fact. That ensures teachers use realistic — also science — vocabulary and resources as much as practicable. Animals are researched within their natural habitats, for example. They are not behaving to people, and they are not wearing clothing. Literature may be enjoyable and amusing, sometimes crazy, but it does not have fairies or super-heroes. Fantasy at Fountainhead can come from the imagination of a child, but the instructor should not force it on the boy. Beliefs and a legacy of customs and legends are valued as things better left to the kin. The Montessori Approach program involves realistic life activities, tactile tools, language (writing and reading), mathematics, and cultural topics.

Realistic Life Experiments ("Help Me Do It by Myself")

Realistic Life activities are the cornerstone of the Montessori educational theory. They include the "motifs for action" that constructively canalize the normal stimulation need of the infant. Practical life experiments are discrete units of research consisting of resources that the infant is likely to encounter in the usage of the everyday world. Each human job must be colorful, appealing, and linked to one of four key fields of its use: Motion control and coordination. Environmental care lessons to learn how to pump, hold, fold, carve, paint, talk, sit, and drive gracefully, etc. Sweeping drills, dusting, cleaning desks, removing drops, watering trees, and so on. Individual love. Exercises to know how to wash faces, shoes, and undress (buttons, zippers, ties, buckles, lacings, bands, safety pins, loops, and eyes), shower, nose blowing, etc. Identified also as Beauty, and Courtesy. Learning to be respectful and compassionate to others, listening to and reacting to other children and adults, taking turns as appropriate, and mirroring the appreciation their teachers and fellow students give them. Even having to walk, stand, and sit respectfully, respectfully preparing things such as meals and demonstrating reverence for the world and those in general.

Realistic life activities include the basic goals of discipline, focus, teamwork, and liberty. As the child is exposed to each operation, executes it by continuous usage, and masters the ability or idea built into the job, these four fundamental elements are simultaneously created. Mastering these skills creates self-confidence by accomplishment pride, and ensures initiative growth.

Dr. Montessori's Sensorial Materials (Educating the Senses) found that by their senses, small children learn knowledge regarding their environment. However, mainstream schooling has traditionally neglected reading or the teaching of the senses. To counter this, Montessori created different apparatuses and practices. Today researchers continue to keep up with Montessori in their debates on the value of sensory integration.

Of such terms as long or short, soft, or light, adults may quickly draw up a visual picture. Children create these abstract comparisons for themselves by using, for example, the red rods, which increase in length from 10 to 100 cm. Dr. Montessori said, "the purpose of the sensory materials is not to provide the infant with new experiences (of scale, form, color, etc.) but to put structure and framework through the numerous experiences that he has already acquired and is still obtaining." In addition to arranging all these sensory impressions, the sensory materials help to organize these impressions. It is incredible to see a four-year-old kid order colorful tiles from deepest red to palest pink because an individual rarely notices the variations in these color gradations. Via this training of the senses, which involves fine motor regulation and hand-eye coordination, and the tactile stimuli along with real-life lessons, the infant is equipped for learning, reading, and mathematics.

Writing and Reading

Dr. Montessori's Language found that children would first begin to write before they learn to read. By breaking down the writing into short, developmentally appropriate activities, young children will quickly learn to write and read. The actual process of writing requires several aspects and is dynamic. The three fingers that support it must carefully balance the writing device; the hand must be able to travel gently over the page, and flexibility must be established to enable the mind to guide the hand to travel accurately. Many of the tasks in the physical existence and tactile fields include as an underlying aim the training of the hand to compose: gripping the knobs of the firm cylinders with the three compose digits, contacting as gently as necessary the rough and smooth surfaces, drawing along the edges and bases of the geometry cabinets, etc. The infant follows the sandpaper letters subtly as he hears the sound of each word, thereby understanding the word phonetically and visually, and transferring it via the sensory mechanism of his muscle memory. He should start constructing basic phonetic words using the mobile alphabet when he learns many letters (a type of mechanical writing — the child normally cannot understand what he has developed at this early stage yet). The other steps involved with writing planning usually accompany writing. It also happens explosively, as the kid accidentally figures out that the letters he has put together really shape a phrase he knows — "f-r-o-g are a frog. I can only understand it! "Then a lengthy time of devouring any term insight accompanies this exploration.

Children at a very early age quickly learn conceptual principles when they are introduced to materials that clearly explain the abstractions they depict. The number rods display the characteristics of "one" to "ten" that no other materials have yet been able to do; sandpaper numbers enable the child to track and understand numerals visually, verbally, and in the muscular-tactile meaning, just as with the letters from the sandpaper. Such things slowly introduce the infant into series numbering; knowing odd and even numbers; the decimal system; principles of addition, subtraction, multiplication, and division; skip numbering (counting in multiples of two, three, etc.); and fractions. In the materials of mathematics, the connection between arithmetic, geometry, and algebra is continually stressed. This base helps children to recognize the role of higher mathematics in later life more readily, and hence they begin to realize its importance for their own lives.

The Children of Sciences have an insatiable interest in the environment around them. The instructor takes advantage of this great learning opportunity by using physiology, zoology, physics, geology, geography, and various world cultures and also history as jumping-off points for environmental and content planning. If the children find a roly-poly bug on the playground, the instructor set up a terrarium with a magnifying glass for a short period to examine the bug before returning it to its natural habitat. From there, the kids might create booklets that explain the roly-poly pieces in exact science terms. This work would combine workflow competencies, design, and writing abilities. Another thing may be to create roly-poly templates in paper or clay. These activities may lead to studying about the variations between roly-polies, which are insects. The instructor may use insect templates for sorting, marking, and counting. And the objects of society are a part of the entire world.

Creativity

The idea of liberty inside boundaries is central to the Montessori process. In this atmosphere, innovation will thrive as children feel secure, valued, and welcomed. A child can explore the possibilities of any material so long as it is used in a manner that does not harm it and is also healthy and respectful of the needs of others.

Knowing the right usage for content stimulates imagination instead of inhibiting it. Much as an artist learns on guitar to create music, and does not use the instrument like a hammer or shield, a child uses red pins, gold beads, scissors, or markers — each object for its own purpose. The professional Montessori instructor is pleased to see a child using a fresh, imaginative content in a meaningful way. Music, sculpture, rhythm, and imagination, excel in each school, along with the Montessori content. Many tasks include different places and hours during the day, but when a child operates "alone, under guidelines," it is also the best time and place for curiosity.

Discipline

Being in a room of many kids and instructors rather than parents provides a child with several different obstacles. In reality, learning to get along in a scenario like this is part of why school is important for young people.

Demonstrate accountability to society by assuming sole responsibility for their actions. In this way, even the principle of justice is created. The children themselves resolve disagreements among children to the fullest degree practicable on the basis of the rules of behavior at school. The teachers will not use corporal punishment, and physical violence by children is not permitted. Teachers work with the implications of an event in both cases, rather than make a judgment about the behavior of the pupil. For example, a conflict about who gets a right to certain content is resolved by the theory that the individual who first chooses the research has the right to use it when completed, without interruption. The instructor may say, "It is now changing to Alice. You could get a change when she puts away the job. Can I give you another piece of work while you wait? "If a child has hurt another infant, he or she is liable for trying to repair the injury to any possible extent — for example, by trying to clean and bandage a wound or by supplying ice for a bruise. The instructor might say, "I can see that Billy is injured. Should we support him? "When an infant makes a mistake, he is liable for clearing it up. The instructor may initially point out the mess and recommend how to clean it up — placing a project back in the box where it belongs or using a sponge to wash a spill. Later, a feeling of obligation in the infant itself triggers the requisite response. The children and teachers express concern for the group by taking moral accountability for their acts.

Development Planes

Montessori's development plans integrated those ideas into a philosophy of child development. Kids advance through four planes during creation, each with distinct physical and psychological evolutions. Consequently, each plane needs the atmosphere to adapt appropriately to deliver suitable learning experiences. The Montessori approach is formulated accordingly based on where the infant is placed in the developmental planes.

Infancy (birth-6 years)

This period is marked by the Sensitive and Absorbent Brain Periods. Those two things function together, creating an unprecedented learning ability. Training is quick and informative. In what is called an involuntary Absorbent Environment, children know through their senses during the first three years of life. Through positive hands-on training, children grow actively throughout the second three years. Learning happens when they can do something alone.

As Dr. Montessori researched the spontaneous engagement of children, she found that children passed through intermittent phases in which they became keenly involved in very particular environmental elements. When children begin increasing stage of growth, new sensitivities emerge and during the first three-year period increase in strength and focus; however, over the next three years, they slowly slip away before the sensitivities of a next phase take over.

Such cycles of heightened attention, or critical times, in the Montessori tradition signify the emergence of opportunities of developmental potential. Kids continue to center their concentration on individual items and events during these intermittent phases of heightened concern, thus avoiding certain environmental factors. -- specific motivation becomes so strong that ' it causes its possessor to conduct a certain set of acts with an incredible outpouring of energy for us' (Montessori in 1949.)

When heightened attention in the midst of a stressful time causes a child to concentrate on the part of the world, Dr. Montessori found the random interaction that resulted to entail a huge amount of effort. In addition, the child is fully integrated into the interaction. If kids are left free to pursue this exercise for as long as they wish, they look relaxed, confident, and content when they are done, rather than drained. Where some people may define this form of child interaction as play, it is considered child labor in the Montessori culture.

When a new vulnerability occurs, if children want to develop the associated 'task' in an appropriate fashion, they need to identify something in their world that is the object of their attention and behavior. If the environment may not encourage a young child to leverage a developmental opportunity indicated by a vulnerable time, the chance will be missed, and it will be far more challenging for the child to achieve the same developmental phase at a later date.

Montessori instructors strive to develop experiences that suit children's needs at critical cycles and thereby promote the development of children at times when their ability to produce the associated accomplishment is at its best, quickly and naturally.

Neuroscientists are also revisiting the concept of the developmentally impaired cycles of infancy and early adolescence. Work tends to support the presence of these cycles, but the consequences for early education remain to be explored. Montessori educators may suggest that crafting a learning experience to a specific level and carefully monitoring the voluntarily chosen behavior of a child within the setting appears to be the strongest approach to draw decisions about whether to address the specific needs, sensitivities, and desires of a particular person.

The Psychic Embryo

The 'psychic embryo' is the term Dr. Montessori used to characterize the post-natal phase. Much as an embryo requires a different, secure atmosphere to 'construct' any of the structures that will eventually work to support existence after conception, newborns require a caring, secure atmosphere to make up any psycho-social 'cell' they will later require to operate in the human community's social and mental existence into which they are raised. For example, the development of the eyes and ears of a child before conception is mirrored by the growth of the visual and aural senses of a child in the immediate period after conception. Whether the psycho-social roles of an adult infant grow relies on the relationship between the extraordinary capacity of the infant to understand and recall, and the content and social atmosphere created by the carers and culture of the child. Children build themselves from the tools available in the world.

The Absorbent Mind

In Dr. Montessori's concept, the 'absorbent mind' is portrayed as a special and effective way small children understand and recall. Small children, she suggests, 'absorb' experiences from the world, and these perceptions shape the internal structure of the under-constructed mind and intelligence. What's more, young people are studying and recalling without realizing they are only doing so because of living without needing more commitment than feeding or breathing! (Montessori, 1949/1982). The absorbent mentality helps the children to adjust to the particular time and position they are born into.

Childhood (6-12 years)

Having learned much of the fundamental skills he would require, this period is marked by consistency. Children develop out of their Absorbent Brain, and through logical thought and creativity know. Children are expected to consider the environment that affects them, how things function, and why. This is the period to identify the most accurate knowledge, as adolescence brings in a reduction in this learning force. The age group's critical time focuses on societal recognition and the creation of a culture of meaning.

Adolescence (12-18 years)

Teenagers show a decrease in motivation at this stage and do not want to be bombarded with knowledge regarding learning. Therefore, schooling will be applied to real-life skills. While Montessori never transformed this stage into a realistic learning method, she conceived of developing schools that were, in reality, self-sustaining families, where learning can arise spontaneously by research on tasks such as cultivating their food, preparing meals, constructing houses and designing clothes. By being autonomous and having to function in peace with others, teenagers will thereby become better able to transition to the adult environment.

Transition into adulthood (18-24 years)

This phase is marked by work development and job beginnings. If, in the preceding stages, the person has acquired the requisite cognitive and social skills, then he would be able to make exact and rewarding career choices.

2.2 Is Montessori A Constructivist Model of Learning

If you are still confused between Montessori and The Traditional Constructivist model of learning, read this chapter for detailed elaboration.

Constructivism is 'a theoretical philosophy that keeps people to actively construct or render their own understanding, and that truth is defined by the learner's interactions' (Elliott et al., 2000, p. 256). Arends (1998) notes in elaborating constructivist theories that constructivism believes in the learner's personal creation of meaning by practice, and that meaning is shaped by the interplay of existing awareness and new experiences.

What are the Constructivist principles?

Knowledge is created, rather than natural, or automatically ingested, the core concept of Constructivism is that human understanding is developed, that learners create new information on the basis of prior experience. This prior knowledge influences what new or modified knowledge an individual will build from new experiences in learning (Phillips, 1995). Learning is an active method. The second idea is that studying is more an involved phase than a passive. The passive view of teaching views the learner as 'an empty vessel' to be filled with knowledge, whereas constructivism states that only through active engagement with the world (such as experiments or real-world problem solving) do the learners build meaning.

Knowledge may be obtained passively, but comprehension can not be, as it must come from making meaningful associations between prior knowledge, new knowledge, and learning processes. Everything knowledge is socially formed learning is a collective task, rather than an abstract idea (Dewey, 1938), something we do together in connection with each other. Vygotsky (1978), for example, believed that the community plays a central role in the "making meaning" process. For Vygotsky, the atmosphere in which children grow up will influence how they think and what they think. So all teaching and learning are about sharing and negotiating knowledge that is socially constituted. For example, Vygotsky (1978) states that cognitive development stems from social interactions of guided learning as children and the co-constructing knowledge of their partner within the proximal development zone.

The aim of traditional Constructivist method is to transmit the already established information, abilities, and expectations of behavior so it can train the children for the potential obligations of the future. The instructor is mainly the significant person in the classroom and offers the stimulus; the setting and resources play another similar function. The program is detached from daily life and does not have conceptual meaning. Students are required to "read" this knowledge, also referred to as "empty slates" or "empty/blank vessels," and bring it back to show that they have become a master at the content. The imaginative, initial thinking is provided very little attention, and performance is strongly dealt in terms of memorized data. Students are inspired by incentives or penalties, which are believed to make learning simpler.

There's a flaw with the definition, however. Since students essentially need to look back at the program, we can say it barely contributes itself to higher-level cognitive skills growth. Since there is never any student involvement in the content being learned, students, for the most of it, merely memorize information to get ahead in the exam and then forget them easily.

Montessori vs. Constructivism

The constructivist philosophy, as suggested by "father of progressive education," John Dewey, is an effort to fix the errors of the old traditional instructive method (i.e., understanding all capitals of the state). The constructivist teacher's job is to guide students articulate their own queries and views and to help students analyze and evaluate their study findings. Constructivists view the process of learning as a cycle of three stages: exploration, implementation of concepts, and application of concepts.

Constructivist philosophy has five main tenants:

- The lessons are constructed over a question that "sparks their interest," which the children make up a hypothesis about.

- The lessons should be of the child's relevance.

- The lessons build on the idea that "less is better."

- Learning starts with simple principles (whole picture), rather than with the specifics. The students form their individual interpretation in such a way that they it understand best.

- Adults view and respect the perspective of their pupils. The constructivist philosophy encourages teachers to practically show a knowledge of the comprehension of the students by answering questions, focusing on to the responses, and answering for detailed elaboration. It is different and in contrast to the previous, old conventional teaching model, which implies that there are correct and incorrect answers (some are supposed to win and some lose) while studying for rote memory and that it is easier to be correct, rather than have intriguing ideas.

- The syllabus and course related tasks are tailored to address the assumptions of the students. There has to be a set dialog with alignment between the queries the students have and what it is they are capable of understanding cognitively for learning to occur. Teachers, instead of teaching and evaluating mediate and review. Authentic assessment inside the constructivist theory framework questions like, "what you know about it," and "what have you actually understood about it?" It encourages interdisciplinary exploration that allows large and questions which are mainly open-ended to be addressed.

The infant begins communicating as the creation causes it to act so. The kid is not growing, but he needs to make use of such inventions. The child will not think that way: "If I want to move from this place to the other, I must begin to improve my walking ability to do so." He will not suggest, "I want to learn language because I can demand for my meal when I am craving it." Nope. The development process comes first, and the human person uses this creation only for a corresponding time. There is also a whole-time where the infant does it itself without the intention of performing the exercise in itself, and this type of exercise involves an immense deal of work on the child's part. And, gradually over time, when the infant grows his thinking capacity, he often gains the willingness to utilize his imagination; the two items go alongside; when his logic progresses, he implements this growth of the capacity of thinking.

Hence we can conclude that the great distinction [between mainstream schooling and Montessori schooling] resides in the personality, vivacity, curiosity, and excitement that the child displays while attempting the work, as well as the ability and approachability along with which he is studying. (Addressed in 1913 by Maria Montessori.) Like Dewey, Maria Montessori became a vital component of what is regarded as the movement of cognition development. Her research as a physician and science expert set the tone for her hypotheses regarding children's "growth schedules" and "active times." She also felt and recognized that there was a need for cognitive stimulation for repeated behavioral (emotional and motor), along with the role that the atmosphere plays in promoting the intellectual growth and wellbeing of children. Like stated in the quotation above, at the moment, Montessori found it pointless to attempt to improve the growth of a child beyond its potential.

Just like Dewey, Dr. Montessori emphasized that experiencing things is not merely passive reactions to the different stimuli present (lessons). "In schools like that, the students are fastened, like butterflies fixed on sticks, separately on his position, the bench, spreading the worthless wings of pointless intelligence that they have gained" (1964, Dr. Montessori). Indeed, her beliefs also foreshadow those of constructivist supporters: "What is known is formed as a complicate set of ideas in the child. Aggressively developed by the individual child itself through a sequence of psychological processes reflecting an inner development, psychological growth. (Montessori, 1965). The theory of Montessori is focused on both biology and concepts of psychology. She introduced many of the concepts.

Montessori along with Jean Jacques Rousseau assumed:

- Knowledge is the basis of learning

- Non-artificial outcomes are mistake management

- The infant is intrinsically pleasant and wants to do research

Montessori and John Locke believed:

- thoughts arise from basic experiences that occupy the blank slate mind of the newborn

- The sensory system works to establish a bond between the two.

- Children in this developmental plane are motivated to set themselves up and immersed in the abilities that push them toward freedom. As they understand to handle their independent lives, learning is guided inward.

At age 6, infants become most involved in language roots and the theoretical universe surrounding them. They want elegant artifacts and fabrics which are aesthetically pleasing. At this point, children are forming their creativity, morals, and critical thinking skills. They would like to know what position they stand in the global universe, hence the concept of Cosmic Education given by Montessori. She strongly assumed it would be inspired by a message that stimulated the child's mind and have consequences that last much longer. She claimed there's a newfound sense of independence, and students are able to make their own choices over what things to pick from. The areas of interest they select prompt them to ask a lot of questions and investigate, and to make new comments. Having several items in the classroom at Montessori enables the learner to develop their own syllabus and curriculum.

2.3 Montessori Lesson Plans

Montessori educators define the task voluntarily chosen by the children as their work. The phrase 'work' implies an arduous task performed to create some form of the finished product, so it might seem out of position in our age were playing, not working, is known in early childhood as 'the basis for all learning' (Waller and Swann, in 2009). If children in our period are free to create via play, it is in no small portion thanks to the work of social intellectuals like Maria Montessori, who advocated for the abolition of child labor at the turn of the twentieth century. Therefore, it is worth exploring what precisely Dr. Montessori intended when she described the children's spontaneous activity as their work.

Dr. Montessori was very specific about the task that she did not consider was the work of girls. For one, she was horrified by the schoolrooms' 'sorry show' that originated after the Industrial Era, and that proceeded to plague the lives of countless small children long into the twentieth century. Huge numbers of children were 'condemned' in such schoolrooms, in her opinion, to sit on uncomfortable benches in dusty rooms, listening to the instructor for a long period. Furthermore, according to Dr. Montessori, the teachers of 'prizes and rewards' used to make children give attention to 'barren and pointless information' lead in 'unnatural' and 'induced' actions (Montessori, 1912/1964). That, Dr. Montessori concluded, was a type of 'slavery' from which kids wanted emancipation. So, the practice Montessori educators term the job of children is definitely not controlled practice. It is essentially a form of practice that many adult people might consider play; however, with two distinguishing characteristics (Montessori.)

- A lot of purposeful work and focus is required.

- It is targeted to potential milestones.

Using the term 'work' to define this kind of practice is a reflection of the importance it gets in schools of Montessori. Montessori instructors discourage something that may disturb or interrupt a functioning child as often as possible since the initiative and attention of the child are known to be reactions to the heightened concern of critical time and, therefore, a symbol of positive growth. Montessori educators claim the word 'job' gives the practice with which children create the value it owes to the adults of the future. After all, this operation can be seen as the most important contribution that every community gives to society

Prepping a Montessori atmosphere for an Infant Group

The household is the first setting for newborns. The bond developed in the first weeks of existence while the baby is snuggled and fed, and the affection that the baby gets from parents and guiders establishes the foundation of confidence and stability in which the entire future of the infant lies. Montessori Assistants to Infancy offer many ideas for parents to establish order and routine within the home, to give the child as much free movement and autonomy as possible, and to set up everyday activities so that the child can join and contribute. For the first time, a little one journeying away from home will enter any of the two Montessori environments designed for children under three years of age.

- For babies with working parents, a Montessori daycare program for infants aged 2 to 12 months is accessible in the Nido or nest.

- When children start moving, they will attend the Montessori Baby Group for children aged 1-3.

The surroundings of Nido and Infant Community are not anything like the more familiar environment of daycare or playgroups. Like the Children's House, a Montessori environment for infants is a miniature world, this time to the scale of even younger kids. Like the Children's House, it is designed to give exciting activities to these very young children and as much autonomy, freewil and independence as available.

The Infant Group atmosphere, like all Montessori settings, is bright and airy, clean and healthy, orderly, and lovely, with plenty of room for children to walk around freely. Since babies and babies use their perceptions to discover the world, there are several textures, such as bricks, wood, glass, and cloth. For their sensory application as well as for security and practicality, fabrics used for soft furnishings such as rugs, quilts, pillows, and cushions are chosen. At the children's height, there are room mirrors and stunning mobiles that capture the attention. Furniture and artifacts are actual, matching the children's size and their strength and ability. There are stairs to ascend, and objects to grip and push to develop balance and gross motor skills. There's a dedicated area for increasing operation to add to the order, whether it's meal preparing, feeding, or changing nappy. Both events are planned, and these tiny children require as little support as possible for parents. Floor beds encourage kids to sleep anytime they want to, and walk about again anytime they awaken, without having to get assistance from an adult. Parents are advised to give children clothing they may put on and take off on their own. Pre-measured portions carefully help the children make meals individually or in cooperation with adults. The emphasis is on letting the kids reveal what they can do on their own. For starters, if children can move, they are not carried; whether children can rise, as they are moved, they are not required to sit down; although children are yet unwilling to take a spoon, parents will not push food into their mouths but leave the spoon in reach so they can pick as and how much to consume. The Infancy Assistant is actively watching, often able to change the atmosphere to enable growing children to discover new opportunities and obstacles and to ensure that the children are not disturbed, excessively-stimulated, or overloaded.

Movements and mind

So far, we have seen Montessori educators perceive the freely selected, simultaneous activity of a child as the work of the child. That research often requires some sort of movement. In the Montessori perspective, human action is a manifestation of the human spirit.

Equality, purposeful activity, and early childhood focus Dr. Montessori contrasted the production of activity in human infants to that of small animals. When young animals, such as rabbits or horses, are born, they approximate the coordination

51

and agility of the species' adults quickly, sometimes almost immediately. In comparison, premature babies have little of the adult strength, agility, and flexibility. Human infants continue to develop mastery of movement through their prolonged infancy. This involves attempts and monotonous practice, whereby children simultaneously impose themselves both mentally and physically. Children make this attempt in pre-school years as they find such gestures as the preceding so interesting:

• lifting, walking and juggling, in other words, rotating the whole body with balance

• engaging individually in the everyday events of the modern society they see around them

• use the hand with consistency and precision

Dr. Montessori stated that while children participate in voluntarily chosen goal-oriented play, intellectual energy and physical action become organized and focused. Over time, if children use their minds regularly to direct their motion, they demonstrate the ability to control both their movements and their thoughts, willingly and independently. In other terms, when their bodies develop the strength they acquire strength over their brains. Children who can monitor their minds can, on a voluntary basis, focus their attention for prolonged times; that is, they have the ability to focus. In Montessori words, this is how they free themselves of their own needs from becoming captives.

More and more children are empowered to get their actions and behavior under voluntary regulation, that is, the more they will guide and govern themselves, the fewer they need to be controlled and governed by others, and the freer and more autonomous they can become. Children take the first initiative down this journey of growth by selecting things that they consider naturally fascinating, that is, a plan that suits the responsive cycles of their era. Once children are on the road, the practice moves them to self-regulation, focus, and independence.

Teaching Social Skills

Every toddler's parent knows that teaching them social skills is not straightforward. That's because even if babies want healthy, enjoyable experiences with others — their own anxieties and expectations get in the way. They can't help wondering — is that child going to grab its toy? Will they bring the truck in front of the other? When the other kid is forced off the cycle and speeded off, can they get away with it?

And the first move to having children grow emotional maturity is to make them understand how to control their feelings, which is the base for interpersonal interactions. The latter helps them learn empathy for others. The third is to help them learn to communicate their desires and emotions without needing to strike.

This ability set would prove more important to the joy of your child's existence than academic achievement, financial performance, or any of our other traditional acts. In reality, emotional intelligence — defined as the ability to control one's own emotions and to connect well with others — will be a key factor in his or her subsequent academic and career performance in your child's existence, perhaps more essential than IQ. And, how is it that you make your kid develop social skills?

Empathize and Sympathize

Children who get a lot of support from adults in their life for their own emotions are the first to build support towards others, and studies have shown that empathy for others is the foundation of positive interpersonal relationships.

Stay close over playgroups.

Most kids strike when they feel distracted through social encounters because they really do not know what to do about it. If you are there, you may ask, "Yeah, Ryan was taking your bucket is that all right with you? Doesn't it? You might say: 'My bowl! "When the kid understands when you're backing up, hitting isn't likely to become a routine.

Do not push kids to partake.

Unfortunately, it prevents exchanging skills growth! Children ought to feel comfortable in their possession before sharing. Alternatively, incorporate the taking turn's principle.

"It is the duty of Sophia to use the pot. Now it is your time. In addition, I am going to make you wait. "

Let the child determine how long it will take for his turn.

If children believe that adults can take a toy away after the adult's vague notion of "long enough" has gone, you are demonstrating picking, and typically, the kid is more possessive. If the kid is able to use the product as much as he wants, he will love it to the maximum and then give it up with a clear heart. If the same kid uses the same product every time, you should purchase a repeat item because either it is such a crowd-pleaser, or you can take different turns.

Help them wait for your kids.

If your kid is having a breakdown waiting for her turn, it is a sign that she has some huge emotions to get out and is taking advantage of the convenient chance. In an effort to shore up their delicate equilibrium, children sometimes get defensive about possession — just like adults!

Empathize: "Waiting is hard, you hope you could use the basket now" and help her up as she is weeping. You will be shocked to see that she actually will not really know about the doll she has been longing for after "showing" you those pent-up feelings and would happily pass on.

Think of compulsive picking.

Often when children snatch, they do not really think about the other person. Do not hesitate to enter, though. Instead, take notice. They are probably playing a game. Much of the way, when one of the kids is upset, you should not worry.

If one child is constantly grabbing, though, then you probably need to intervene. Children would also snatch whatever the other kid has, then drop the item and continue to the next one to replace their own miserable feelings. Such emotions require support.

So gather all your sympathy, place your hands on the disputed item and ask, "Would you like the truck? "In addition, look at the vehicle the kid is using. "Is that all right with you? "If that is — great. You do not need to be the arbiter of equity.

Assertiveness teaches.

If your child often allows other kids to take stuff from him and often appears sad, ask, "You do not want to give it up, do you? You might tell, 'I am really playing with this.' "Experiment with him acting this out at home and demonstrating it with teddy bears. You will need to be his "face" while he interacts with others before he learns the language skills.

Slow down. Make sure to reflect while talking to your toddler, then stop to allow him a chance to answer before jumping in. When your kid knows she has your full attention, Ecclestone suggests she is expected to communicate with you through noises, movements, and vocabulary.

Say something crazy

You will gain the attention of your child and provide an incentive for her to connect just by being dumb or doing anything unexpected. Seek to place her in a waterless pool, or leave her cereal bowl bare. She would have to convey that something is wrong with you, whether it is by movements, noises, or sentences. Then, speak to her about what you intend to do to get it changed

Rather than celebrating communication in the abstract, help her learn what is actually cool about it.

Research suggests that children do something most when we encourage sharing — but only while we are listening! They simply do it fewer when we are not, so our appreciation does not owe them much incentive to share beyond the moment of our focus. Instead, encourage her to make the decision of sharing in the future by making her see the impact of her choosing: "Look how delighted Michael is that he gets a turn with your car." If you follow the strategy of having children have a turn for however long, however, they wish, they gladly transferred the desired object to the other child at the end of their turn. They get to know how good it feels to send. So having children manage their turns is the perfect way of promoting cooperation and kindness.

Kids will get a chance to put away their most exclusive things before visitors come over if they do not want someone else to play with them. Using this practice as a way to demonstrate why the visiting child would obviously want to interact with Junior is other toys, even as Junior enjoys the toys at their homes with his peers.

Set the physical violence to reasonable limits.

"You should tell us how crazy you're without harming. Come; let's tell Henry how crazy you are because I'm going to comfort you." "You should yell NO and stamp your foot as hard as you want. You should yell, 'Mum! 'And I will still support.' Babies, like our arms and legs, are entitled to their emotions, which have a way to only exist in humans. Yet all people, including the small ones, are liable for their arms and legs and emotions about what they are doing. Our responsibility as parents should be to teach them safe methods of self-management without becoming harsh, which also makes the children more aggressively violent.

Giving the children language for their feelings is never too early.

Emotion marking is the first step of the brain's capacity to perceive it mentally, rather than physically.

"When you concentrate hard on your tower, it's so painful; then it falls like this. "The huge dog's bark is frightening, but you're protected on this side of the fence, and I'd never let it harm you. The exception to that is when kids are in the throes of a major emotion, where so many words will drive them out of their hearts and into their heads. Only tell your kid he's healthy at those moments, and save the phrases for later.

Remember that there is typically pain or anxiety behind the rage.

Recognizing such emotions is often more successful in transmitting wrath than merely marking the wrath, which just appears to intensify it. "I hear Jimmy is very angry with you. I wonder if you are sad because he needs to be interacting with someone else right now. "That's even more important when children say," I hate him! "Hate is not a feeling; it is a position.

"Right now, you're so upset at your brother that you sound like you're never going to figure out anything with him. That is what it means by the word hate. Even we feel that way when we are very, very mad, even at those we love. We are a team, and we are just trying to hash it out. Let us go and tell your brother that he hurt you by pushing you off the swing, and how angry that makes you feel. Continue incorporating the notion of understanding how people behave as early as possible.

Hold cool

Research suggests one of the most effective things parents can do to help children know how to control their feelings is to remain calm. During the turmoil of their tumultuous emotions, children need to perceive their parents as a "keeping environment "— a secure haven. If you will remain calm and soothe your girl, she can gradually learn to soothe herself, which is the initial phase in learning how to handle her emotions.

Keep in mind they are young

Only because James bites a playmate does not mean that he is going to be an ax-murderer. It's important not to encourage negative conduct against others, but that doesn't imply you're not giving understanding — and the confidence your child can gain. "Sometimes, even the children get angry at their peers. When you grow older, it will get better to know how to manage yourself as you feel angry, and you can sort through problems. "Children deserve to learn from parents because they are not evil people.

2.4 Ideal Montessori Learning Environment

The significance of a Prepared Maria Montessori's "prepared atmosphere" is the idea that the setting should be structured to promote the child's full autonomous thinking and discovery. There is a range of actions, as well as a lot of movement in the trained area. An instructor from Montessori represents the infant as the preparer and tactician of the world and is responsible for preserving the climate and order of the planned community. A structured atmosphere allows the growing child the freedom to thoroughly explore their abilities by tactile materials that are appropriate for growth. The materials vary from basic to complex and from real to theoretical, which conform to the age and skill of each boy.

Montessori classrooms are structured to deliver lessons, activities, and resources to suit the individual child's developmental needs and interests. It's necessary to remember that not every child is involved in any lesson possible. That's why children can pick the experiences they instinctively gravitate toward.

Many parents can ask what separates Montessori childcare from the regular daycare or preschool center. For example, as soon as you reach the typical childcare center, you'll find that it's most definitely busy, noisy, and messy. In the opposite extreme of the continuum, as soon as you step into a classroom in Montessori, you will find its calm, quiet, and organized. You may ask why the two childcare programs vary so far from each other. The distinction resides in something called the structured setting by Dr. Maria Montessori.

Montessori Classrooms

A Montessori classroom is typically a large, open-minded space with low shelves, various tables' sizes that comfortably seat one to four children and seats that are suitably designed in the classroom for the children (Figure 1.2). While not uncommon still, one of Dr. Montessori's inventions (Elkind, 1976) was creating furniture that was suitably made for the children who might need it. Practical Montessori classes often have communities of at least three years of age; all six years of primary education may be integrated with smaller schools.

The classroom at Montessori is organized in sections, typically separated by low shelving. -- the field has "materials," the Montessori word designating academic items, for research in a specific subject field (art, music, math, language, science, etc.). That contrasts sharply with traditional schooling, where learning is primarily extracted from texts. On the Montessori Elementary school, books are increasingly critical as instruments for learning, but even there, hands-on activities prevail. Dr. Montessori claimed that deep focus was necessary to help children achieve their true self, and that deep focus arises in children when interacting with their hands, and objects.

In providing a clean look, Montessori classrooms often contrast with other traditional schools. In a wardrobe, additional supplies are held out of reach and moved in and out of the school, when children appear to be eager for or no longer in need. Each material has its position on the shelf, and after usage, children are required to bring each element back neatly in its position, ready for another boy. Attention to the environment is strongly respected, with consideration for the interests of others. The focus is often expressed in how the classroom is organized by teachers. Materials are thoughtfully arranged both inside and around topic regions, and the structures make common sense. Children are not allocated seats but are free to travel about throughout the day at any tables they want to operate.

They may even work on tiny rugs on the board. Children can choose for themselves, whether they want to work alone or in groups established by themselves, even when the instructor is giving a lesson. With very few exceptions, all lessons are given to individuals (most often at primary level, 3- to 6-year-old level) or small groups (most often at the elementary level, 6- to 12-year-old). When the children are ready for them, lessons are given; the instructor will write on the board or announce the expected lessons of the day early in the day so that the children can know what to expect. Care is taken that the purpose is not to exert power over the kids, but merely to warn them so that they can prepare their day appropriately.

Education at Montessori is structured to the heart. This often throws people back at the preschool stage. They reach a Montessori classroom, and it is very calm, unlike the preschools they usually see. Children operate individually or in communities in a peaceful way. And it organizes their jobs. They focus, carry out tasks in a sequence of actions that the instructor or other children have shown to them. Research shows that better child results are consistent with organized settings, but the level of order will make the parents feel insecure. The products on the shelf are intended to draw the attention of children and to teach lessons through repetitive usage. Much of the items are constructed of wood and are either organic or painted in chosen bright colors since they have been shown to draw children. Any content has a primary motive for being in the classroom; most even have many secondary reasons. Montessori instructors watch children at work, not offering assessments to determine competency, observing that children are utilizing the resources correctly. It is believed that proper usage would produce comprehension. Teachers revisit lessons where children seem to have misused a material and therefore do not derive from it the instruction that is meant to be imparted; new lessons are offered where children seem to have learned material and to be ready in a series for the next.

There are different methods of utilizing the items, which are demonstrated to the children in the classes, in accordance with each piece serving a primary function. With Metal Insets, which consists of standard geometric shapes made of metal, children are not supposed to make music; the materials break down essential practices into a sequence of structured moves that kids learn individually before putting them together to do the main activities. These measures also represent indirect planning; children are unsure of what the steps lead to, however, the instructor is conscientious, and methodically introduces the materials. A clear example of how Montessori learning continues is in writing and reading education.

What Is The Prepared Environment?

Throughout her book The Joy of Childhood, Dr. Montessori defined the goal of the prepared environment as follows: "The first aim of the prepared environment is to make the developing infant independent of the parent whenever appropriate." Thus, the prepared atmosphere is one of the central elements of the Montessori theory. The learning atmosphere and all that the child comes into touch with will promote independent thinking and discovery, according to Dr. Montessori.

Primary elements of Prepared Community

Independence — The right of choice is one of the critical goals in a Montessori-prepared setting. This is accomplished by allowing the child independence to experiment, free expression, free social contact, and free intervention from others.

Montessori believes in allowing our little one's more freedom to select their daily activities. During the meantime, we, as teachers, will be observing and advising them whenever possible. It enhances cognitive capacity (the awareness, reasoning, studying, and assessing process).

Framework and order — The theory behind this concept is to represent the framework and order of the cosmos so that the infant can internalize the meaning of its environment and thereby begin to make an understanding of the world around him.

Beauty — Making the atmosphere welcoming for learning is also essential. Therefore, the mood will be wonderfully and simplistically crafted in such a way as to invoke calm, tranquility, and harmony. The workspace will always be well controlled and uncluttered.

Culture and Truth — Dr. Montessori claimed that children would be motivated by religion. That is why teachers at Montessori often send the kids out into nature to use natural learning resources in the prepared setting. Such products are not synthetics or fabrics, but genuine timber, concrete, bamboo, structure, and glass. The tools should also be actual and child-size because the child can interact with the materials on its own without discomfort and without needing to rely on the adult for movement assistance.

Social atmosphere — The prepared community will promote social progress through the fostering of equality of contact. Montessori schools encourage the creation of a sense of dignity and empathy for others while rendering children more socially aware.

Academic Atmosphere — after all of the aforementioned ideas have been met, Montessori educators should be able to reach children in the educational setting that enhances the child's whole temperament and intelligence.

Creating an Ideal Montessori Environment at Home

Being autonomous involves being able to do something about yourself, being able to make your own decisions, and handle the effects of those decisions on your own. It merely implies 'not hanging from' anyone else or whatever. Dr. Maria Montessori witnessed small children struggling to become autonomous during their long lifespan. She believed the push toward independence that encourages young children is the same force that reinforces their growth. For this purpose, the classrooms at Montessori are designed so that children can choose their tasks individually. In these practices, children acquire not only necessary information but also how to take control of their own interests and their world on their own. Often, they know how to create relationships with each other. A Montessori classroom also referred to by Montessori educators as the 'world,' is specifically built such that a children's group can behave and communicate as individually as possible.

Montessori Activities for You And Your Child

Montessori-focused activities are interesting and unique, helping to stimulate independence and self-trust for your child. Here are a few basic and exploratory activities which you can try anytime. The Montessori curriculum teaches that student-led learning will encourage children to function at its autonomous level and speed. This, together with the instruction offered by devoted instructors, promotes cognitive, mental, social & physiological growth of your preschooler. No doubt a lot of parents love that style of learning!

If the pre-school of your child is already closed, or whether you only want to introduce the Montessori method at home, this is a perfect place to continue. These projects are only a Launchpad, enabling your child to try whatever areas and topics he or she is most anxious for. Follow her on. After all, she is the owner of the learning experience.

Water Play

It is a perfect opportunity to experience the surrounding world. Children learn essential lessons to float, fill, weigh, and sweep. There are several ways to integrate water related plays into your everyday life, which goes above the normal method of simply enjoying in the bath. Here mentioned are some ideas for you to begin with:

- Scrubbing: By using distinct scrub brushes, sponge like tools, and cleaning items, your child will learn about textures. They're willing to clean animals, walls, rocks, and even pinecones.
- Misting plants: Give them a watering that is child-sized, or have them go for the bigger version of it. We recommend you set the hose for gentle watering to prevent an unforeseen water fight.
- Bubbles: You can squirt soap inside a water-filled tub, pan, or cup. Let your kid blend it with a whisker, and watch the bubbles become bigger.
- Dishes: Your child is not too small to assist in simple cooking tasks. Set them up with a footstool or a tower standing at the bath. Start with plastic, metal, or wooden boards, tassels, and cups. It's cool if they only have fun with the dishes, and with the water — you can drop it all into the dish washing machine later.
- Measurement: Using cups to move water between jugs or bowls. Keep count of the number of cups a bucket or a tiny bowl needs to fill.

Food ingenuity

Indeed, little children will assist with food preparation. Only ensure it's enjoyable, imaginative, and play-oriented. Combat picky eaters? Okay, we've noticed that children are more inclined to choose to consume food when they help cook a meal. Although that may be suitable for every child, particularly young ones, it's worth trying! Below mention are a few things that you can try in your kitchen:

- Spread: Jam, butter, peanut whisk, jelly, or even hummus can be spread on crackers. Don't panic if something falls apart, that's an area of learning.
- Cutting: Let your children practice slicing softer fruits like melons using a butter knife.
- Peeling: Ask your child to attempt peeling an orange, and then hand it to stop.
- Squeezing: You can create the lemonade yourself. Have them by the side and push out the pieces. Having a mess is great!
- Dehydration: It is fun to see fruit move from normal to crisp the shrunken slices. Besides, using a dehydrator is safe for a little boy, as there is a different usage, unlike a danger in traditional stoves. (Yet it is also perfect for adult supervision.) Blending: let your kid choose items to place into the blender. For them, you should run it, but let them practice putting it in the cups.

Outdoor Exploration

Playing outdoors does not have to be restricted to sliding down slides, twirling, and playing tags (though these are also great activities). There are countless possibilities of allowing the children to invest some time outside.

- Gardening: having the kids interested in growing their own food helps to cultivate a wonderful interest in adulthood. Mark off one garden field as your own, letting them choose their own plants.
- Puddle play: That does not mean you cannot go outdoors just because it is rainy out. Get some fun rain boots and go leaping puddles!
- Treasure hunts: Create a list of items that they need to find — like a stone, a smooth rock, a yellow herb, etc.

- Outdoor art: drawing on leaves, creating pinecone handicrafts, putting flowers into a scrapbook, painting with mud – there are countless possibilities.
- Musical wall: Outside, you can hang a variety of things — pots and pans, old forks, tin cans, chimes, and even metal plates. Get some sticks, and begin to make music.
- Stick family: Locate and call a set of sticks. Find a place in your yard to build a house for them, with a mound of leaves for their nests, a rock circle for them to cook, and some acorns for them to mumble on. Every day check on your stick mates.

Life Skills

A child learning his shirt buttoning is a life skill. The theory of Montessori interweaves realistic knowledge with freestyle games. That gives your child thumbs up on on being an adult that is efficient, positive, and independent. Always doing stuff as if lace up your shoes for them is good. However, if they can do anything on their own, let them. Only make sure you allow ample room to acquire new skills.

- Dressing: Begin by picking one object at a time and putting trousers on, for starters. Continue to focus on it and empower your child to do it alone. Then switch on to shirt putting. Definitely follow videos providing advice for the daily world.
- Washing up: Making sure General Grooming is included in the routine. You can also use a cloth to wash your preschooler's face, scrub his toes while in a bath, or use a shower brush to get all those trying to reach places like his back.
- Reusing: Your child will assist by rinsing recycled cans, throwing them in the bin, and even having you roll them out into the driveway. Talk to him about why reuse and recycle stuff is important.
- In an emergency: Kindergartners will begin knowing essential facts, such as their home number, address, and how to dial 911.

2.5 FAQs about Montessori

As a parent, it is very likely that you have many queries related to Montessori by this point. Hence, this part of the chapter is completely dedicated to all kinds of questions a parent can have regarding the Montessori Method.

Are the services recognized at Montessori?

The Montessori instructional approach is well established. The Montessori programs are based all over the world. In addition, many new childhood development and education textbooks are referring to Dr. Montessori's important contributions to the field of child education. Montessori applications are also recognized through different programs and societies. Of these societies, the most notable are the American Montessori Society and the American Montessori International. It is beneficial to be certified through one of these communities, as it provides parents with an assurance that, as Dr. Montessori intended, the Montessori syllabus be being professionally adhered to in all its facets. Bringing credentialed also guarantees that the proper materials are being provided and that the correct number of teachers have accomplished their Montessori training program.

Q. How are the children in a Montessori system disciplined?

Any Montessori system participants are surprised by how calm, friendly and well treated the kids are. Montessori programs are notorious for their children's self-discipline. What is especially noteworthy about this is that the approach does not require bullying, threats, or deception tactics. The kids do not consider their teachers as strict or evil. Energy or control methods are not required. What happens is that the children feel that they are fulfilling their needs. They want classrooms and coaches. They believe the instructor is responsible for them and is a source of support. The kid clearly wants to be taught how to fulfill his/her wants in a constructive way. Unacceptable behavior declines through this phase and eventually disappears. This makes the classroom an extremely pleasant place for both the teacher and the children. The secret to the cycle is:

- Development of an atmosphere able to fulfill the children's developmental requirements

- An instructor educated in optimistic, meaningful strategies to supporting kids

Q. The Montessori curriculum is geared to up till what age?

Montessori products are available and are meant for use for children up to the age of 12. There are a few middle and high schools in Montessori. Montessori, though, mostly produced resources directly during the years of elementary school. That was because she saw the need for specifically crafted products, especially for the younger kids, because the older kids should have the opportunity to benefit from widely accessible.

Q. Why do Montessorians use the term "work" to describe activities for children?

Dr. Montessori's profound appreciation for children is expressed in her philosophy of curiosity and discovery. She recognized that the students were in a self-construction cycle, constructing themselves constantly from inside. The specific classes, tools, and way of being in society (aka, "work") help the normal growth of the growing infant.

Q. What is the development of Montessori children, and are they good after leaving the Montessori environment?

There are no "classes" given in the school of Montessori. Evaluation is by portfolio, including the assessment, including record keeping of the instructor. The instructor closely observes any child's academic success, joy, development, and enjoyment of learning, and addresses it with the parents. Recent findings indicate that children from Montessori are well educated for their adult life – academically, psychologically, and emotionally. When exposed to a conventional school setting, they usually adapt well. In addition to doing highly on standardized exams, Montessori kids are graded above standard on factors such as following instructions, handing in on-time assignments, listening closely, utilizing practical knowledge, demonstrating maturity, posing challenging questions, displaying a passion for learning and adjusting to different circumstances.

Q. What about special kids?

The Montessori classes are built to support all children (those who are "gifted" and those with learning difficulties) at their own speed achieve their maximum potential. A classroom of children of different abilities is an environment where everybody learns from each other, and all participate. In comparison, multi-age grouping helps each child to reach its own rhythm in relation to peers, without feeling "fast" or "behind."

Q. What specialized qualifications do the instructors at Montessori have?

In addition to a bachelor's degree, teachers with Montessori certification have completed the course ranging from 200 to 600 hours of class and a year-long practical experience. The teaching includes concepts of infant growth and theory of Montessori as well as practical applications of Montessori tools in the classroom. There are training centers in Montessori in various places around the United States and around the world.

Q. What is the principle behind the Montessori approach to early childhood education?

Montessori is an instructional philosophy focused around the idea that learning will operate through, rather than against, the child's existence. Learning would also be focused on the child's empirical research and the subsequent perception of growth and learning processes.

Q. Are Montessori faith schools?

Some are, but the rest are not. Any Montessori schools work under the auspices of a church, temple, or diocese, much as most schools, but most are autonomous of any religious association.

Q. Are infants covered by the Montessori program?

Children under the age of two are extremely capable of learning about the environment around them. The Montessori Infants Program has been designed specifically to help the development needs and interests of young children. The most critical aspects that children acquire in the Montessori Baby Curriculum are activity control, good social skills, language learning, and basic conceptual principles that qualified them for the Toddler and Preschool Programme.

Q. How do teachers at Montessori meet the needs of so many different children?

Good instructors help the learners get to the stage that their hearts and minds are free, and they are ready to know. Students are not only inspired by having good grades in successful classrooms, as they are by a profound enjoyment of learning. As parents know the learning styles and temperaments of their own children, teachers, too, develop this sense of each child's uniqueness by spending several years with the students and their parents.

Q. Why do the classrooms at Montessori have mixed age groups?

Parents frequently wonder why Montessori classrooms divide children into two or three-year age ranges, while through their birth year, primary schools divide pupils. The main explanation for this is that mixed-age programs are promoting learning to mimic, a good sense of belonging, and empowering children to function within their growth level.

Q. How long will it take to for my child to settle in?

It takes a specific period for each child to move into a new childcare facility. Some kids decide on the same day when others can take more than a month. For children attending three or more days a week, they are expected to relax faster than children attending fewer days do.

Q. How do Montessori kids compare to the kids from other programs?

Children in a Montessori curriculum are frequently ahead in grade level by many years. They are generally involved in anything they like learning. They are usually polite, compassionate, collaborative, and respectful of their properties as well as others.

Chapter 3: Montessori & Child Psychology

Montessori products were systematically developed within the curriculum in an educational setting, with particular attention to the needs of children depending on the developmental period they were moving through and in the assumption that handling tangible artifacts helps to improve awareness and critical thought. Many of Montessori's views can be linked to psychological theories and child psychology. This chapter has elaborate explanations on child development from a psychological perspective.

3.1 Understanding Child Development

Reports and research suggest that children may profit from Montessori concepts emotionally and cognitively. A 2017 analysis compared Montessori students with regular schoolchildren between the ages of three and six reported that Montessori-educated students demonstrated "elevated outcomes" in many ways, including

1. Social Cognition

Social cognition relates to the manner in which an individual collects and retains knowledge for later re-use. This research showed that the children of Montessori tended to grow social awareness quicker than their typical peers. In other words, across the three years, Montessori pupils displayed substantially higher rates of academic performance relative to their conventional school peers.

Nevertheless, one thing the researchers noticed was that it took some time for this to become clear. Children were originally monitored and found to be on equal learning standards in the mainstream and Montessori programs. However, the more the Montessori participants stayed in the curriculum, the higher the difference between the two classes of academic performance becomes.

2. Confidence in Learning Subjects

Researchers in the analysis observed that children participating in the Montessori program were more likely than their conventional classroom peers to display optimistic emotions towards school and learning events. That does not suggest they did not enjoy typical childhood things like playing football or watching TV. Nevertheless, in comparison to all other learning practices, Montessori kids were more likely to show an enthusiasm in literacy and other intellectual endeavors.

3. Mastery Orientation

This concept applies to the trust a child has in the abilities to answer and solve a problem, such as a puzzle. Children in the Montessori system were more inclined to choose difficult puzzles when they presented a variety of solutions, and they showed greater faith in their abilities to solve a challenging puzzle, too. The researchers then concluded and theorized that this might be in part due to

Montessori's focus on intrinsic gratification as the primary incentive for a well-doing job, rather than the measurable incentive scheme that is sometimes found in a typical classroom setting.

Activities to Boost Toddler's Development

Check Out Textures

Toddlers are tactile learners that appreciate feeling, hearing, and experiencing the environment around them. Using a dark marker to draw alphabet letters and/or numbers on poster paper; then decorate your tot with textured things like sandpaper, shells, cotton balls, pasta, and pipe cleaners. Grabbing the letters allows children a chance to experience the way a letter is being shaped. For those little ones that begin to type, their fingertips will play with a letter form before finding a writing utensil. Say the letters and numbers out loud every day while your kid is brushing his fingertips through them. Earlier the practice is expanded by making a poster that spells out his first name. Your child will soon spot these letters on banners, advertisements, and posters.

Start Measuring Up

Learn how to weigh your child using daily objects. While a ruler is known as a popular measurement device, playing with months, seasons, or time of year to stimulate the learning method. Get your child lie on the lawn in the fall, and then line up apples next to her to determine how many "apples tall" she is at those ages. Or decide how many "Legos big" the sofa is in your house, or how many "wooden blocks long" the refrigerator is in. Figure out how many books your child would need to cover your room for extra fun. Just calculate when you lay down the numerous items, and your child will quickly calculate and weigh in many different ways!

Mark Your Home

Pick either one or two things in your house to be numbered, such as the refrigerator, windows, and furniture, and then change the branded products every few months. Allow stickers the same size and use a simple script, so that children can quickly distinguish them. Write, print, and cut off individual words; then use the blue painter tape to add them to artifacts (which enables quick removal). You may even add the terms on items on index cards and attach them. Labeling helps kids to realize that everything has a series of specific icons to write down and define. When your child is older and now ready to understand letters, show her the letter "lamp" starts with, and remind her to locate the mark that ends with "L." If she is still too young, pick out various letters, and expose her to the symbols. Strengthen the idea every day, and your child should be able to autonomously define the terms over time.

Sing Vocabulary Words

Build this ability by making humorous melodies with rhyming words and count to ten, or performing simple, popular songs like the Alphabet Song or "The Itsy Bitsy Spider." "In the pre-reader years, kids acquire an average of nine new words a day," tells children's author Eugie Foster in Pam Allyn's Writing Life / me for your Baby. "Parents have a greater chance of seeing that possible if they build environments for children that are like the nets of dream catchers, catching precious words and their vibrations," says Allyn, who is also LitWorld's Executive Director and founder.

Encourage automobile music, performing at home, and at bath time. If your child is undergoing daycare or pre-school, ask the instructor for favorite songs from the class and reinforce them at back when home. Teach grandma and babysitters songs such that this lighthearted practice includes all the significant people in your child's life. Your child will begin learning by song as she narrates letters, figures, weekdays, and sections of the body in melodic tunes.

Number Your Mornings

Build a calendar grid of 31 boxes on a piece of poster board, and then leave the room at the top to attach signs for each month. Write down the week's days through top and bottom 31 cards of numbers 1 to 31. Add Velcro to each card's back, then to each of the 31 poster cases. Hang the calendar at the stage of your child's eye and add a monthly sign on the first day of each month and the number 1 symbol on the correct day of the week. Challenge her the next day to locate the number 2 card, and work out the week's day. You can even aid in performing the

Days of the Week album. Your kid will start to grasp the calendar and the numbering scheme. In addition, according to Allyn, "routines provide children with support in areas that adults sometimes overlook about."

Pin-Up Pictures

Place photos of friends and relatives in your child's space on a bulletin board to build word recognition and enhance recall. Write the names of individuals on sticky notes (include titles like "daughter," "dad," and "cousin") and mark them at the bottom of each photograph. Refer to the terms regularly, particularly at a family reunion. Delete any sticky notes from the photographs, as everybody is more comfortable with your child. Often, read books on brothers and sisters, or aunt and uncles, and encourage your child to describe every of the listed family members. As your child develops, expand the game by building a family tree that includes names and pictures — making this a continually evolving piece of work of art in your house.

Introduce Organization

Cultivates the helpful nature of your child by cultivating structure and organization in your household. Even if it can slow down tasks and chores, parents will accept the price. Connect your household operation to the mark by storing toys, clothing, plates, and kitchen products in different places. Render the cycle a guessing game when you placed items in their numbered bins and drawers.

Ask kids where other things go ("Where are your toys going? Where will your shoes be stored?") Alternatively, put forks in a sock drawer or play in the fridge and encourage kids to correct your "mistakes." They will love to reorganize for mum or dad, who does not seem to know where the cups go! According to the writers of Common Sense Discipline with Toddlers and Preschoolers, Bridge A. Barnes and Stephen M. York, "these exercises offer you a chance to start educating your small children about obligations, supporting others and becoming part of a team."

Plan a Scavenger Hunt

Children become natural explorers, and they want to explore. Scavenger hunts can be developed or conceived in preparation on the spot. Check the store for products that are one particular color (like purple) or search around the house for items in one form (like a circle). If your child wants to support, pick three things for her to select from when questioning, "Which object is pinkish? Which object is a triangle?" Extend the game on the Mark Your Household by organizing a scavenger hunt for various branded products, or encourage her to check the bookshelves for a particular letter, phrase, or number. You should always say you could not locate the carton of orange juice or a pair of shoes. Take your child on a pleasant quest to localize the house products.

Start to learn the area by pointing down the basic store, fire department, petrol station, and other important locations. Discuss the specifics of certain community staples when you visit each spot. It involves who goes there, the intent of your visit, and the things within you find. Then draw or print pictures of these locations and position them together with their information on index cards. Return to those "neighborhood" cards the next occasion you are out together with your boy. For example, if you drop by the dry cleaners, ask your child to find a corresponding "neighborhood" card and ask him a question: Purchase dry clothes or pick up washed clothes? Who works in there, a firefighter or a cleaner? Extend the area experience by organizing visits to a nearby fire department or a police station. Strengthen this practice by showing them the Sesame Street popularized the song "The People in Your Neighborhood."

Every toddler's parent knows that teaching them social skills is not straightforward. That is because even if babies want healthy, enjoyable experiences with others — their own anxieties and expectations get in the way.

They can't help wondering — is that child going to grab its toy? Will they bring the truck in front of the other? When the other kid is forced off the cycle and speeded off, can they get away with it?

In addition, the first move to having children grow emotional maturity is to make them understand how to control their feelings, which is the base for interpersonal interactions. The latter helps them learn empathy for others. The third is to help them learn to communicate their desires and emotions without needing to strike.

This ability set would prove more important to the joy of your child's existence than academic achievement, financial performance, or any of our other traditional acts. In reality, emotional intelligence — defined as the ability to control one's own emotions and to connect well with others — will be a key factor in his or her subsequent academic and career performance in your child's existence, perhaps more essential than IQ.

Work of Montessori, Itard & Seguin

Analysis of intellectual retardation and other developmental problems in children by Itard and Seguin Montessori led her to the research of two French doctors and psychologists, Jean-Marc Gaspard Itard (1774–1838), and Edouard Seguin (1812–1880).

The research of Itard and Seguin by Montessori has had a significant formative impact on the growth of her system of education.

Itard, an Otiatria nurse, has operated with adolescents who were deaf and hard of hearing. He was instrumental in converting the form of clinical assessment used by their medical doctors to infant assessment by the instructor.

His first notable case was his excellently publicized care of "Aveyron's wild kid," a feral man, seemingly abandoned or lost as an infant, who had been discovered living with animals in the mountains. The kid, around twelve years old, had no language, and had no functional skill. Itard had undertaken to educate the boy to teach him in real-life skills and voice. Although he had some modest improvements in training the boy, there were no encouraging findings in the experiment at Itard. A robust student of restricted skills, the boy defied much of Itard's attempts.

Itard's experience with the "wild guy," and his research with mentally disabled children prompted him to hypothesize that humans were going through unique, definitive, and essential periods of human development. Itard was not the first developmental thinker to emphasize the significance of social growth phases. The Roman rhetorician Quintilian (approx. AD 35–100), the Czech theologian and scholar John Amos Comenius (1592–1670), as well as the French intellectual Jean-Jacques Rousseau (1712–1778) all, had recognized the critical value of educational growth. Itard came to his theories through observational study of real children as opposed to those earlier educators who focused their ideas regarding creation on introspection or contemplation.

According to Itard, children encountered their developmental periods by participating in behaviors appropriate to the specific time and for which they were biologically and mentally trained. However, abnormal children, particularly those who were physically or mentally severely impaired, tended to miss the maximum potential of the developmental stage and were left with deficits that affected their further growth.15 He deduced that children needed to encounter the activities suitable to their developmental stage at the right time or bear the consequences of continuous and cumulative development.

Itard's research focused upon many significant themes: culture and human knowledge, and the extent to which human intellect is acquired or taught. There may be a distinction to the fictitious "noble warrior" of Rousseau, Emile, who learns mainly through simple sensory experiences, separated from civilization. Though Emile of Rousseau develops into a compassionate natural guy, itard's Introduction research was very different for the real wild child. Like the laissez-faire and permissive teacher of Emile, Itard was searching for unique forms to teach the boy. In coping with intelligence, Itard observed that knowledge, though a provided one, evolved at the right moment of growth by getting the correct experiences.

Itard's research had greatly influenced Montessori. A specialist such as Itard, Montessori has been qualified in clinical assessment. Readily embracing Itard's theories of scientific testing, she named his actions "the first behavioral psychology attempts." Seguin, a psychiatrist who had practiced psychiatry with Itard, consulted with psychologically ill children and implemented his techniques at the Hospice de Bicetre, a teaching school for children removed from Paris' insane asylum.

Seguin claimed that facilities for children with disabilities would become educational, rehabilitation centers, and that all scientific and pedagogical expertise could be used to address the state of impairment. He has continually emphasized the child's physiological assessment and evaluation as a method of diagnosis, care, and schooling. Seguin created a collection of academic apparatuses and tools to educate the senses and enhance the physical abilities of mentally disabled adolescents. Seguin introduced many methods that Montessori would incorporate in his research with these youngsters, such as basing teaching on developmental phases using didactic curriculum tools and preparing youngsters to practice functional tasks so they could gain a degree of independence. Seguin's groundbreaking special education initiatives became a spark that incited Montessori to dig further into schooling. Montessori derived two ideas from the research of Itard and Seguin: first, that intellectual disability demanded a different kind of education and not just medical care; second, that this specific kind of training was improved by the use of didactic resources and instruments. Nevertheless, the teacher's practices were moral in the education of mentally disabled children and indeed all children, in that it was essential to operate on the child's heart, which was a "kind of hidden key."

3.2 Child Psychologists & Montessori

The four aspects of Montessori teaching that were most out of line with the early 1900's ideas included Montessori's focus on mental or cognitive progress, physical input, the child's reactive growth stages, and the child's natural involvement in learning. Cognitive growth was also a key priority among educators. However, Freud's observations of the human being's mental and sexual growth, and his influence on his actions during his life, had a remarkable influence on the educational scene in America. For the first time, modern philosophers and educators have understood the child's instinctual urges and desires. Perhaps it was expected there could be an intense move away from academic learning and into an effort to interact with these recently identified trends explicitly in the classroom. Impressed by Freud's exploration of the mayhem that can push down repressed animosity and impulses, educators and parents developed a more permissive approach towards conduct that had not been accepted before. Even behavior that was physically destructive was sometimes accepted. It was thought that kicking dolls, hitting cement, tossing over blocks and toys, and smashing items to sort out their repressions was ideal for girls.

It is only lately that many parents have been conscious that their liberality and lack of control in this and other ways have contributed to children becoming undisciplined and depressed. Montessori felt that child behavior, which was physically abusive, was destructive. Far from helping the child feel better about himself, she noticed it left him more depressed than ever before. She did not tolerate such actions in the school, thinking that it was not part of true independence. In its place, she stressed the desire of the infant to explore himself and his willingness to react favorably to his surroundings through the excitement of learning and imaginative activity. She assumed a reduction of moral expectations or academic growth would contribute only to poorer schooling and culture.

If schooling is to be an assistance to society, it cannot be achieved by emptying the schools of intelligence, character, discipline, social peace, and, above all, independence.

Charles Darwin

Darwin's evolutionary philosophy, centered on natural selection, has left the early 1900s American culture with a conviction in xed knowledge. The importance Montessori put on early cognitive learning was completely out of line with the philosophy. Why worry about cognitive development if intelligence is a constant, not subject to modification of the signals? The accepted predetermined development theory was also a legacy of Darwinian influence. If the human embryo follows the development of the species in its formation, subsequent growth, including cognitive development, will well continue in predetermined stages, regardless of external inducements.

Arnold Gesell

Arnold Gesell is well known as the foremost literal depiction of these stages in the growth of the child. The resulting approach to child rearing has been one of "letting the child outgrow it" whenever unpleasant behavior. As one father told me, "Since he was two years old my son [now eighteen] has been going through 'a stage!' "Montessori claimed that the infant would have some factors in his life otherwise else he will not grow normally; so, however, when there are times of destructive behavior, that is because the infant is attempting to convince us that there is no great need for his. She noticed that this form of behavior vanished as the child started to concentrate on his job and gained self-confidence and self-acceptance by exploring himself and his skills. Both the trust of xed ability and the fixed growth hypothesis was given a deathblow in the 1940s as American psychologists started to shift their focus to the impact of early life factors on children's intellectual development. Freud's findings in the early 1900s had sparked curiosity in infancy and early childhood. However, the emphasis was on development, which was emotional, not intellectual. Following World War II, our emphasis on the cognitive development of the young child also began to our own.

It was reported that the children were suffering from extreme retardation in orphanages and schools. This happened despite the fact that outstanding physical treatment had been given well to the babies. Sixty percent of the two-year-old children did not sit alone in one such institution; eighty percent of those four-year-olds could not move. There was one clear finding regarding these institutions: these children provided little to no tactile stimuli. There was no vibration, next to no movement to watch, the walls were colorless. The lack of sensory stimuli in the premature environment apparently had an effect on these children's development.

Donald Hebb

Psychologists have also been conducting tests to explore the sensorial restriction consequences of certain environments. One of such psychologists was Donald Hebb, a man whose research and philosophy changed the direction of contemporary American psychology in a substantial way. Experimenting first with animals like rats and then gradually with dogs, Hebb found their adult problem-solving ability to vary considerably in the richness of their early environment. Hebb wrote his Behavior Organization, a novel theorizing on his experimental research, in 1949. This book provided Montessori's approach to early learning and environmental stimulation with the rest psycho-theoretical basis. Before a discovery that was made, it was commonly assumed that the brain should work via basic patterns or associations for stimulation response. Such relations were created for repeated interactions and comparisons to evolve and become lasting mental patterns. The functioning of the brain resembled a telephone switchboard. (It was on this commonly established principle of brain structure and function that Kilpatrick had based his criticism of the philosophy of transfer-of-learning and, thus, one of his key challenges to Montessori education.) This hypothesis of brain function did not sufficiently account for the Hebb effect, although some were ending in the laboratory in the light of early environmental influences. Hebb developed a much more critical theory of the neurological structure and brain processes that considered those phenomena. He argued that "cell assemblies" representing images or ideas are formed in early learning, and that these assemblies are joined into "phase sequences" in later learning, which facilitates thinking that, is more complex. Thus, later learning would depend on the wealth of the cell assemblies formed earlier.

Observation by Montessori of the child's spontaneous interest in learning was also supported by Hebb's theorizing. Any behavior was previously believed to be driven primarily by instinctual or homeostatic needs (the organism's need for a healthy physical and chemical state). If this were true, if no such motivation were present, the organisms would be quiescent. Physiologists, on the opposite, have recently identified that the central nervous system is continuously involved independent of external or endogenous stimuli. Hebb theorized that in addition to the already recognized motivation based on instinctual drives and homeostatic needs, there needed to be an intrinsic motivation for behavior. H did some of the critical research that would support this modern hypothesis. Harlow, F. In three different experiments, he observed that monkeys could and will learn to operate puzzles where no other incentive but the appearance of the puzzle itself has been ordered. Real learning had been demonstrated as once the puzzle had been mastered, it worked awfully and persistently. Harlow also showed that, rather than promoting, the usage of hunger-reducing incentives simply undermined incentive. He found that, as soon as they were finished, monkeys who had been rewarded with food for working their puzzles ignored them. On the other side, the unrewarded monkeys always continued investigating and exploiting the puzzle after it had been completed. Nearly fifty years ago, Montessori came to specific findings on the children's inner drive for learning through studying children specifically rather than animals in the laboratory. She had developed a classroom protocol based on this inner incentive, totally discarding the gold stars, special rights, qualifications, etc. that are now standard use as inducements to learning in classrooms today.

McVicker Hunt

Another visionary in the field of motivational learning is McVicker Hunt, who is particularly relevant to Montessori. He found that babies acquire habits of remembrance, and would attempt to repeat them after six months of age (crying to try the return of mother). The child often slowly becomes fascinated and may deliberately pursue the enjoyment of excitement within a known sense. "A major source of pleasure lies in finding something new within the context of the familiar." Novelty becomes a tool of motivation, then, if the old corresponds correctly to the new. The enticing novelty tends to be an ideal disparity in this partnership between the moment's input of knowledge and the details already accumulated in the cerebrum from experiences with specific circumstances. The child will be frustrated if there is too much excitement or incongruity; if it is too little, he will be bored. Hunt called "the matching problem" the dilemma of finding the proper amount of each for any specific child at a given time.

Chapter 4: The Ultimate Parenting Guide

Becoming a new parent can be very exciting yet frightening at the same time. It can in fact get as scary as possible especially when it comes to the health of your newborn. As a new parent, it is essential that you realize you will make mistakes, but you will have to forgive yourself. Remember that, as a parent again, you are the primary caretaker of your child and that you will learn from your own experiences and take on responsibility rather than from others' take on parenthood. However, it is also completely normal to experience this roller coaster of emotions as there are plenty of ways to educate yourself about your little one. And, this chapter of the book has got you covered; starting from hypnobirthing to introducing you to baby sleep-training and feeding techniques and other effective parenting methods, it will provide you all the basics you need to become an expert parent.

4.1 The concept of Hypnobirthing

On its own, the word hypnosis implies "a treatment through which individual encounters proposed improvements in feeling, vision, thinking or actions." One specific marketed type of hypnosis is referred to as Hypnobirthing during the conception phase. Although this general concept has been around for decades, hypnotherapist Marie Mongan in the 1989 novel Hypnobirthing invented the precise word: A Celebration of Life. The theories are inspired by Dr. Jonathan Dye and Dr. Grantly Dick-Read, the pioneers of early "random conception."

Hypnobirthing, at its core, intends to help a woman deal with any apprehension or discomfort she might have around conception. It requires different methods of calming and self-hypnosis to help the body recover before and after conception and childbirth. Using breathing exercises and self-hypnosis, parents will support each other through a system that can help you conquer your worries and learn to disregard the painful birth myths that continue to spread and intimidate us during pregnancy.

The idea is that birth can happen faster and more painlessly once the mind and body are in a completely relaxed state because the body is not fighting the natural process. Hypnobirthing ideals seek to merge mindfulness and birth hypnosis, with the goal of eliminating any of the anxiety around childbirth and offering moms-to-be the encouragement and trust they need to make giving birth into a genuinely positive experience. Hypnobirthing provides moms-to-be with the courage to deal with discomfort, to aspire for an orderly birth (making reference to inducements), and to be comfortable if the delivery is not scheduled, for example, when an immediate C-section is required. Hypnobirthing's emphasis is on the relation and imagination of mind and body and looks at how self-hypnosis may help birth mums deal with the discomfort they feel in childbirth.

Relaxation is a term for the Hypnobirthing game. Yet how do you fall into a Zen-like condition amid all the theoretically turmoil of contractions? Well, several methods can be used, such as relaxing and levers.

Controlled respiration

The Hypnobirthing Midwife discusses two other methods of ventilation. You breathe heavily through the nose in the run, then through the nose back. Inhale into the four-count, and out to the seven counts.

The second is close in methodology. You adopt the same method of deep breathing, but lengthen the inhalation to the count of seven, and hold the exhalation to the count of seven. It will serve to stimulate your parasympathetic nervous system by relaxing in this manner, offering you some soothing vibes.

Concentrating on positive thinking and words

Concentrating on happy thoughts and expressions is another helpful tactic. You can use "surge" or "shock" for a more optimistic perspective instead of using the term "contraction" to explain the tightening throughout labor. Another way is replacing membrane "rupture" with the term "release."

Guided visualization

Other methods involve guided visualization, where you might imagine things like a flower opening to help calm the body, then use music then meditation to calm more. The aim is to give birth in a condition similar to daydreaming by utilizing such strategies. You may: be more conscious of what is happening to you and be able to come and go out of hypnosis when you please becoming more comfortable, holding the body out of the fight-or-flight state that may be triggered by the new atmosphere of a birth room to be more able to handle endorphin release pain and stress hormones By regulating pain and stress hormones, the body may let go and submit completely.

Related Hypnobirthing-like techniques are often called the Mongan Method. It is known to be the "first" form, which contains five classes that are 2 1/2 hours long, for a total of 12 hours. There are several accredited teachers in the Hypnobirthing worldwide. The key concept of this approach is that once the body is calm, extreme discomfort will not have to be included in the labor. Participants practice different methods of self-hypnosis and calming, including directed visualization and respiration.

Hypnobabies is another way of getting hypnosis during the cycle of conception. This is focused on the Painless Childbirth Program, which the master hypnotherapist Gerald Kein created. This technique has some key differences, although similar to Hypnobirthing. It depends on different approaches to deal relieve discomfort vs. purely calming strategies. Such methods include strategies such as hypnotic compounding (repetition) and even somnambulistic (sleepwalking) "professional school" hypnosis.

Hypnobirthing may:

- Reduce labor, along with confidence in the birthing cycle. In fact, birth hypnosis may help to shorten the first stage of labor. This stage requires both early and active labor where, when the cervix expands, contractions get longer, deeper, and closer together.
- Lessen the desire to interfere. A 2011 analysis of research found that Hypnobirthing could help promote natural birth, and people utilizing hypnosis may not need as much oxytocin augmentation. A 2015 report showed that just 17 percent of Hypnobirthing's Reliable Root moms had cesarean deliveries relative to a general 32 percent average in the United States.
- Manage discomfort normally. Hypnosis can also help if you are aiming for medium-free labor. Fourty six out of eighty-one participants (51 percent)

did not use any pain medication in one 2013 study and reported their maximum pain level on a 10-scale as just 5.8.

- Offer them a feeling of power. Women have also indicated feeling more confident and in charge of the 2013 survey. As a result, they became less fearful of labor and conception.

- Good babies lead. Apgar ratings, which is the method for measuring babies in the minutes after conception, could be higher for babies raised utilizing Hypnobirthing.

- Help those women who have had trauma. In fact, Hypnobirthing may benefit birthers who have encountered distress around conception or who have a general apprehension of labor and childbirth.

If this is your first kid, and you are scared, excited, concerned, or just want any support to aid you through the birth process. Alternatively, whether this is your fourth baby and your previous births have not gone as planned and left you feeling nervous or depressed. Hypnobirthing applies to all! It can assist in any kind of birth, whether C-section, VBAC, home birth, college, at the car's back!

The course is intended to attend moms-to-be with their birth companion (husband, child, girlfriend, relative, family member). Your birth companion is the one you would like to be at your birth with you. If this is not approachable for you, even then you can still do the course on your own and still get a beautiful birth from Hypnobirthing.

Popular misconceptions about Hypnobirthing

- The hypnosis connected with hypnosis is a type of mind regulation or brainwashing.
- Hypnosis sends you to a deep state.
- A person who was hypnotized has no free thought.
- If you are hypnotized, you cannot do
- Regular activities and functions.
- When you are hypnotized, you do not realize what is going on around you.

Is it possible to hypnobirthing?

Hey. You are not going to be in a coma, or fall asleep, despite the name. You will be conscious of everything that is going on around you, and you will feel completely relaxed and in control. Do, however, remember that problems are not avoided by hypnobirthing.

How can I know about hypnobirthing?

Ask your midwife regarding lessons or seminars on hypnobirthing, since the NHS provides various courses around the world. These can not only help you but also help your family understand more about how hypnobirthing functions in more depth, what happens to your body through pregnancy, what your birth partner can do to support, and, among other items, what antenatal exercises you can do. In courses and seminars, such as extra audio content, you can typically get supplemental content for self-study.

If you are unable to join a course or choose to learn yourself, then you have other choices, such as CDs, DVDs, software, podcasts, and books explaining the methods of hypnobirthing.

When should I start training on hypnobirthing?

Following your 20-week check, the optimal time to book a course is, but it also depends on the quality of the courses in your field. Some NHS-run hypnobirthing courses, for example, can only begin from 28 weeks. Sessions generally last around two and a half hours a day, with four or five lessons over a month's duration.

If you are going to have your baby at a hospital, at a birth center, or at home, hypnobirthing will help you have a happier birth. The strategies you practice in hypnobirthing can only support to keep you feeling in charge, no matter how the labor progresses.

4.2 Baby Sleep-Training Techniques & No cry baby solution

Does your kid have to be rocked to bed by you — or getting up while it is still midnight looking for a breast, a drink, or a cuddle before going back to bed? If your little one is at least four months old, then it might be time to begin sleeping.

Because of that age, babies can — and should — fall asleep, or fall back to sleep by self-reassuring. If you are dreading sleep training (also known as sleep teaching), remember it is always done quicker than other parents expect, and it does not even have to require tons of crying.

When people add to sleep the word "Montessori," it always refers to the growth of freedom during sleep and bedtime. It is important to remember that Dr. Montessori rarely wrote about sleep and that there is no particular solution that all parent (or teachers) in the Montessori model identify with. The key idea is to focus on children being encouraged to obey their hormone sleep window to enable them to self-regulate themselves. Montessori sleep strategies may be useful for trouble sleepers and easy sleepers, as long as you select a system in which you are confident and which is a good match for the temperament of the infant.

Tips:

- Hold to it for a week or more.
- Do not expect everything to function in three days or shorter, some adjustments, and some kids need to adapt at least a couple of weeks.
- Do not allow sleep or penalty a result. Keep it nice. Lots of affection, cuddles, and routines and practices that are calming help make bedtime simpler for children and parents. Ignore the kid as in all things in Montessori.

Floor Bed

The most commonly debated sleep system for Montessori is the floor bed, a crib- or kids-sized mattress positioned either directly on the floor or on a small bed frame. The principle behind this is that children can enter (or exit) their beds safely at any moment, which allows the bedroom to be completely child-safe. This is a perfect situation for some kids, and for some, it is just too much space. (In addition, there is nothing to suggest that if you decide to co-sleep, you cannot make your own bed a floor bed!)

Playing to Sleep

Another idea is "play to sleep" that encourages kids to have access to books and games at bedtime and offer them the right to choose when they are ready to sleep. There are also certain guidelines, so everything is special for each family.

Stimulation

An essential feature of Montessori-style bedrooms is that they do not believe in themselves over-stimulate. The rooms themselves will allow for peace and relaxation so children will indulge in hours of play inside them. Any items that would match the day may need to be withdrawn or changed during the night, such as stereos, shifting furniture to prevent injuries, etc. Montessori is compassionate and serves the infant above all others. When they show that they are willing, we motivate and teach children concepts and responsibilities. Many children require support more than others, so although it is the individual choice of each adult, the Montessori approach takes into consideration the children's wishes so preferences; children are not pressured to meet living arrangements or demands that they feel uncomfortable or disturbed by. That's not to suggest whether a kid gets a choice as to whether or not they're going to bed — they don't — but instead, whether a child feels uncomfortable going to sleep without a light on, with a parent present, etc., we understand that pressuring the child to adhere to our (well-intentioned, well-informed) bedtime arrangement may be counter-productive and doesn't appear as encouraging to the infant. It can help to think about it as eating: we do not let kids pick whether to feed or not, but we do not compel a kid to use a spoon that is not packed. We include the spoon as an option to display them, but we will not sit to watch a child not eat because they are not ready to use a spoon (or do not feel prepared to do so).

It is also necessary to insert some routine into sleep — as in any part of the day. Routine is comforting because they become more relaxed because secure relaxing into their bedtime as children can foresee just what will happen next.

Before Getting Started

Montessori First-time

It's important that even before you even think about "training" your baby to fall asleep on their own, make sure you follow a regular schedule and put them to bed each night at a consistent time (hint: usually better early, typically around 7 or 8 p.m.). It's a smart idea to try and put them down drowsy, then get up whenever you can, just to get them (and you) habituated to it, even if they fuss a little. Be sure they've been up for a decent period of time before bed (an over- or under-tired infant may have difficulty falling asleep), and set up a relaxing and regular bedtime routines, such as a meal, bath or relaxation accompanied by pajamas and stories or songs. To stop letting the kid equate the feeding with falling asleep, specific experts suggest feeding at the beginning of the day. Ideally, during your bedtime routine, your baby should not be beginning to nod off at some point. "You just want to make sure your kid is healthy for the night," says Montreal-based counselor Pamela Mitel man, who specializes in young adolescents and babies. Be conscious, too, of getting adequate exercise and relaxation to fill their daytime awake times, Garden says. "When they are awake, infants tend to be going in all manner of directions, not only sitting in a bouncy chair," she notes.

Here is how and when your baby should start sleep training to help everyone get a good night's sleep.

1) Sleep training no-cry-the fading method

For sleep training with no controlled weeping, the fading technique (a.k.a. gradual retreat) means just doing what you have done so far, and gradually minimizing the contact, you have with your child during bedtime.

The sleep guru and bestselling author of Kid Secrets this morning, Jo Tantrum, offers her top tip saying: "help your kid know how to sleep without a sleep aid" For example, if you usually put them down to sleep once they have gone to sleep, you'll put them down right before they fall asleep with the fading-it-out approach (FIO). If they wake up and cry, then take them back. If you rock them down to sleep, try to prevent doing this gradually. If they weep when you stop, rock them again a little bit, but keep trying to minimize that. Try to replace this with a dummy if your child sleeps on the boob, or get your partner to take the child to bed instead so that they stop affiliating breast time with bedtime. It is a method that is slow, but it can be achieved

2) Minimal contact sleep training method

This method is also known as the pick-up / put-down method and is a more gentle way of the sleeping train. That helps with the parent sitting with the baby until they fall asleep while attempting to lessen the touch, not holding the baby in your arms, for example. Place them in bed, pat them, shoot them, and try to get them back. If they scream, then again, you may pat and shush. If that does not work, then you can pick them up and put them down when they are quiet again.

They have to get used to putting themselves down. The entire idea is only taking up the kid for support then setting them down for the night. Try to keep the contact minimized. You will stop picking them up at some point, and just pat them until you can finally managed to lay them down at bedtime and let them sleep alone. We like that method, and so do babies. At first, it is tiring for the parent and might take much longer than any of the other methods, but it's guilt-free!

3) Sleep training Ferber technique

This system, developed by Dr. Richard Ferber, is also regarded as the technique of cry-out sleep training or the form of check-and-console.

If you have placed your baby in bed with their calming bedtime music or night-lights, you leave the house, and when they complain, you come back, touch them, and soothe them with phrases like "there, there," or "goodnight kid, go to sleep," or your choice terms, before you go. When they scream or complain, you go back in, massage and soothe them again; hopefully without picking them up and then leave again before they fall asleep. If they start crying, you should adhere to the same plan, adding one minute per time before coming back into the house.

The Ferber method's aim is to remind the kid that you are still there, but now its bedtime, so it is time to sleep. This technique is derived from a more severe variant of the Ferber System, and the somewhat divisive, the Extinction Approach, also known as the Cry it Out (CIO) form of sleep training. Marc Weissbluth developed this, so it means bringing the kid to bed, saying goodnight, and then leaving them there to sweat it out before they go to sleep. Many experts and parents highly criticize this method and consider it unnecessary, as there are many other ways of getting a child to sleep alone through the night. That said when they are at the end of their absolute wit, a lot of parents turn to this method as a last resort, with excellent results. If you can stomach it, getting your child to sleep alone through the night is a beneficial and quick way, often within a few days.

The aim of the CIO approach is to let baby stress and weep alone before she ends up sweating herself out and falling asleep alone. You may end up needing to let the baby cry it out at the beginning for 45 minutes to an hour until she goes to sleep, but it differs from baby to kid. Many parents who seek the technique of crying it out see their kids screaming fewer and less over the first three days until their weeping stops approximately anywhere between the fourth until seventh evenings. Eventually, infants will either whine or screech a few minutes of protest — or just fall asleep peacefully. Whereas it depends on your infant and the ease with the process to know whether to let the baby cry it out. Babies are usually able for production to sleep around 4 to 6 months of age. They will sleep through the night by around 5 to 6 months without needing to feed, making it a perfect time to test out the CIO system.

Note that your older baby may already have equipped you with feedings, cuddling as well as a return to your bed to react to her nocturnal cries. Around six months, infants are wise to the idea that screaming always contributes to being picked up, swayed, or eaten — a strong incentive to continue to do so. When that is the case, then baby and you may need any adjustments to the sleep routine. However, if they get the impression that you do not accept their actions, many will give up the game of weeping, typically within three or four days, often longer.

4) Form of sleep training chair

The chair system is a way to let your kid think you are there because it is always bedtime. A milder variant of the Ferber process, you are dressing the kid for bed and setting them down every night following the same procedure, taking a chair and staying next to them before they fall asleep. This strategy will take longer than other approaches as they will want your help if your kid sees you there, so you will have to stop. You should hug them every few minutes if they weep before they calm down. Try not to make eye contact, and if you see the baby scream and do not react, it would be rough for both of you. It is not fun watching a baby cry and doing nothing about it, and that is the same thing the child will ask. If you have perfected them falling asleep while seated next to them, the next step is to push the chair farther and farther forward, until you are totally out of the house.

5) The hybrid method of sleep training

No one size fits all. Some infants respond to dummies, while others do not. Some may like to be swaddled, while others may not. There is no right way, and every parent has to choose what is correct for them and their baby. There are no specific rules of a method for hybrid sleep training. It is just about working for the intuition. This hybrid method allows you to choose what is right for you. You may choose the relieve and comfort method for 20 minutes, then move on to the chair method for another 20 minutes, before proceeding to the Ferber method.

Remember that kids are going through phases, and even a big sleeper may have sleep regression, so, at certain times, you might have to go through sleep training all over again. If you want to make changes to your bedtime routine, gradually make them and lighten the baby into it. The key is consistency with whatever works for you.

Stand up, set down method. This strategy in sleep training includes you moving through the usual cycle of your baby's bedtime and placing her to bed drowsy yet wakeful. Wait a couple of minutes, when and where she starts screaming, to see how she slows down. Otherwise, go back to pick her up to soothe her. Place her back in the crib or bassinet, until she is quite enough.

Repeat until the kid falls asleep. Just be mindful that this form of sleep training will take a long time, which would demand a lot of discipline.

Tips

Sleep training tips the following sleep training suggestions can help make sure a smoother transition to dreamland: establish a bedtime routine no matter what method you are trying to use. Follow a coherent 30- to 45-minute children sleep routine to help your little one transition from awake to sleepy time. If she falls asleep in the breast or bottle, resume that feed in front of the shower or books, so you can put her to bed whilst she is waking.

Time to fix it. It is not the time to play with baby's sleep when his or her life has undergone a recent disturbance (a relocation, new nanny, ear infection, travel.). Wait before things stabilize until you try sleeping preparation.

Know when you have an exhausted kid. Watch for signs of sleep, such as yawning, eye scratching, or grumpiness, which can occur every night at around the same time. It is important to put your baby in bed when she is sleepy but not overtired, as overtired babies are more likely to sleep or wake up early. Place the kid up full. Sleep training is focused around getting the kid to fall asleep in her own — an experience she will not learn if you cradle her to sleep into your arms until she is moved to the crib.

Wait time for your reply. On the first groan, do not rush into the baby's room. In the night, babies make many noises, including weeping, and then fall back asleep. A nodding-off infant may wake up to any little noise or scream, or it can disrupt her attempts to soothe herself.

1. New Child? Support configure the "global clock" of your infant by introducing your kid to clear signs about the 24-hour day outside.

Like older adults, babies have sleep patterns or natural processes that commute every 24 hours, about once. You may think about such patterns as a clock that functions internally, there is a catch: no pre-programmed clock arrives. When babies are raised, their inner clocks are not aligned with the sunlight and darkness external 24-hour period. Babies need time to get in sync. Luckily, we do not have to sit passively to see that happen. We cannot, in reality, be inactive. Babies rely on us for help. Studies suggest that babies respond better when parents send them the correct "time-keepers" or external signals about the hour of the day. So reveal your baby to natural light and get your baby involved in your daytime activities' designed to stimulate the hustle and bustle. Guard the kid against sensitivity to artificial lights as evening comes. As I see below (see baby sleep tip # 2), light is a signal which tells the brain to postpone the onset of night sleep.

2. Use bulbs (or filters) that block the blue wavelengths when you need artificial lighting at night.

If you replaced both electric and artificial light sources at night, you and your baby would possibly consider sleeping easier. Yet complete blackouts are not a practical choice for most of us. When we decide to indulge in evening sports, what should we do, including reading? What do we do when we need a diaper change?

Happily, not all light wavelengths on the inner clock have the same effect. Yeah, white light (that is produced from both fluorescent and incandescent bulbs) has a detrimental impact on sleep habits, and the impact is highly important for small children.

However, one portion of white light — the blue part of the continuum — seems to be responsible for most of the problem. If we can obstruct that part of the light spectrum, the negative effects of nighttime light exposure could be minimized. A low watt, the amber bulb is capable of protecting your baby from blue wavelengths, yet providing you with enough light to perform infant care at night. Similarly, blue light filters can reduce the risk of sleep due to nighttime viewing of electronic screens.

3. Help your baby be settled: create a period of comfort, joy, and mental reassurance the hour leading up to bedtime. When we are anxious or irritated, none of us sleeps well, and babies are no different. So take action to ensure your

kid feels protected, comfortable, content, and valued before bedtime. Try pursuing a schedule at bedtime (Mindell et al. 2015; Mindell et al. 2017).

Look for your own emotional state because of its contagious stress. Babies become more distressed with distress from their careers (Waters et al. 2014; Waters et al. 2017). In addition, if you sense negative feelings in your infant, combat them with reassurance and nothingness.

Studies at assessment say that this creates a difference. Parents who respond soothingly to the emotions of their children report fewer problems of infant sleep, and this is how it works regardless of the sleep arrangements in a family. If children share a bedroom with their parents or sleep elsewhere, when their parents are alert and attentive, they sleep better (Teti et al. 2010; Jian and Teti 2016).

4. Learn the art of stress busting — for your baby and for yourself. A baby who is very easily annoyed or becomes distressed is hard to soothe. This post on tension in babies in Parenting Research provides insights into what triggers babies. It also offers evidence-based advice to keep the babies happy and safe emotionally. However, what if you feel too stressed out for reassurance and calm project? Or far too depressed?

If it is, so you are not lonely. Caring for a baby can indeed be very worrying, troublesome, and even exhausting, especially when you yourself are sleep-deprived, coping with childbirth trauma or struggling with an excessively crying baby (see baby sleep tip # 10). If you are weak in your mental condition, check for postpartum depression and keep your psychological wellbeing a priority. Postpartum depression and postpartum stress are very normal, but many parents are still privately suffering. Discuss your choice with your psychiatrist.

5. If your kid does not seem to be asleep at bedtime, do not try to push it.

Getting bossy does not make children any sleepier, which makes them more hyperactive, if anything. In addition, you do not want to link the kid to a clash with bedtime.

6. Look out for those lengthy, late afternoon naps and seek to extend the last bit of waking until bedtime.

If your baby is not sleeping until late at night, the first rule is to guarantee that, your baby is not subject to bright lights until bedtime (baby sleep tip # 2). Next move? Test the duration of your baby's naps. For infants, naps do nice stuff, but infants are like us: late naps will set off the drowsiness they might normally have at bedtime (Nakagawa et al. 2016). Then see how you can prolong the period your kid spends up during the least productive portion of the day. When researchers tracked parents who used this advice, they found that babies were beginning to need less help sleeping at night (Skulldottir et al. 2005).

13. 13. Do not feel under pressure to burp or diaper your baby if your baby is waking up.

Something you would not want to do while your infant sleeps — or is about to doze off — is to jolt her up with unnecessary treatment. Could you wait, then? That seems probable.

Researchers find no proof of a new review of more than 70 children that burping has proven helpful to babies. It did not make them cry less, and indeed, it increased the chances of a baby spouting after being fed. (Kaur et al. 2015). In addition, an earlier finding shows that the feeling of a damp diaper does not activate babies (Zotter et al., 2007).

14.14. Get reasonable ideas regarding sleeping patterns for your kid?

What is the perfect time for bed? Your kid will sleep for how long? When does your baby start sleeping through the night for long intervals?

If you knew the answers to those issues, it would help you escape traps — and anger without use. For example, if your baby will not sleep the way you should like it to be, it is simple to believe that you are doing it wrong. New parents sometimes worry that if their young infants wake up multiple times at night, there is something developing awry. Night waking are always completely natural.

Parents may even make the error of scheduling the incorrect bedtime to seek to push their kids to fall asleep at a time when their inner clock is out of alignment. As noted in tip # 4 of baby sleep, the resulting conflict can create lasting problems with sleep.

In addition, parents are sometimes overly complacent about certain things — like a baby's nocturnal vampire-like schedule. If you believe that there is something you could not undo, it will become a promise that fulfills itself. You cannot use effective techniques, such as infant sleep advice on light signals. This helps to learn about the normal course of development of infant sleep and the wide range of variations that healthy babies can show.

Frequently Asked Questions about Sleep-Training

Can you sleep train for shorter sleep like naps?

The same overnight sleep management technique can be extended to naps. If you want to cry it out, or Ferber, bear in mind that a large part of the nap may be gone after 30 minutes of screaming. Moreover, you would want to put a cap on crying (say, 10 to 15 minutes) before you find some way to get your baby to sleep.

How long would it take for the sleep training?

Most infants are taught to sleep after three or four nights with strategies such as Ferber or cry it out (save a couple of minutes with fussing or wails before nodding off). Some methods of training — especially bedtime fading, the chair approach and pick up, put down — will possibly take longer, and for some babies, certain approaches will not function at all. Be faithful to the sleep-training approach you have selected to give it a chance to function for two complete weeks.

Is the teaching on sleep cruel?

Sleep has a negative reputation with those seeing raising an infant as an insensitive way to. Sleep is not about plunging a newborn into a crib and keeping it there until the morning after.

Of reality, most professionals warn against making a baby scream for longer than 15 minutes, and not all of the sleep strategies discussed above support that. There are plenty of other strategies to help the kid sleep through the night. Sleep training does not have to be associated with crying, it is not cruel, and it will help you and your baby tremendously.

Why train your child to sleep?

Even like we educate our kids to feed, drink, exercise, and talk – all the essential aspects of a human's everyday existence, so we have to educate them to sleep. Sleep is a big part of living. Even as adults, if we are disturbed by our nightly sleep and have trouble falling back to sleep, it could make us tired, grumpy, and disturbed during the day too. A safe sleep schedule is something that will always help a child well in their everyday lives as they develop. Sleep training can take some time to get the hang of and needs commitment, discipline, and energy, but in the end, it will be worth it.

How do I choose the right method for my baby and me?

One of the main aspects of sleep training is to find the strategy that works best for you. Ultimately, you are the only person who understands what your (and the baby's) ability to sob is. When a process for you does not look appropriate or seems too "intense," do not do it. Start with a gentle plan you are at ease with.

Keep in mind that you and your partner could have different levels of comfort and tolerance. Starting tiny is better then moving on to a less friendly approach if appropriate so you can know what you are happy with and what really won't fit for you and your family. In the end, the best method for you and your family will be the one you can change to suit your needs and comfort levels. There are several various sleep training approaches to pick from, although the most common strategies are described above as one or a combination of one of the five. You may find that one of these methods sounds like it is a perfect match for you, OR you may find aspects from every plan you like.

You may also have learned of the "sleep feeling" or the "sleep lady scramble," as opposed to a specific system, these are actually separate sleep training programs. Typically, though, they implement or function with the same principles that we discussed above.

The scale of sleep training approaches from gentler to less gentle when studying the numerous approaches of sleep training to assess which one is correct for you, note that growing kid and family is special. What one mom swears by, swears off another parent. If you use your instincts to choose, a system you and your baby know would be happy with, you will get the most benefit from sleep training.

How can I ensure successful sleep training?

Sleep planning for any family can look a bit different, based on which approach you want to adopt. To be effective, the numerous strategies need specific approaches from the parents. Tip to Melissa: take notice! Having a list of how your kid has done in the sleep training would be helpful when you are too exhausted to know how long they have been sleeping the night before.

Dream Feeding

Dream feeding: An evidence-based guide to help babies sleep more extended Dream feeding has been described as feeding a sleeping baby, as promoting the baby to sleep for longer. The word was often used to define any big meal that is scheduled to occur shortly before the parent falls asleep (delivered during sleep or waking time).

Are these effective measures? There is justification for believing that they might give you more quiet sleeping time. But dream feeds alone probably play only a modest role in the development of infant sleep. The most effective path to improving advanced sleep habits is to integrate dream feeds with other sleep-friendly activities.

Here is an outline of the subject — the meanings, the proof, the pros and cons, and the questions frequently asked.

What fuels dreams?

Tracey Hogg, who used the word for the very first time, describes dream feeding as feeding a young child while dreaming. In a very gentle way, hold your sleeping baby in a feeding position to accomplish this and try to enhance the rooting reflex by stroking the baby's mouth and offering your baby a breast or bottle. Several babies will eat without waking up in this way (Hogg and Blau, 2005).

Although some people make specific usage of the word "vision feed." For, e.g., Harvey Karp relates to intentionally waking a child as : "Vision feeding is when you wake up your kid to eat once more before you switch in for the night" (Karp, n.d.).

Others use the label "dream feed" to portray any effort to "tank up" your baby before you go to bed by yourself. It's not clear whether the kid is sleeping or alert. What is important is the meal arrives only before the parent rests. So with both these meanings, that's the basic denominator — the notion of having a kid to take in a large meal until you doze.

Newborns are quickly and often awoken by the empirical rationale for dream feeding, in part, because they are starving. If you start to sleep shortly after your baby has "boozed up," you may get some more time before your baby wakes up again.

In addition, every bit helps, particularly if you can sleep uninterrupted for a minimum of 4 hours. Our brains are built during the first few sleep stages of the night to target the most restorative period of sleep — NREM3, or intense, slow-wave sleep — And if only one part of your nightly sleep bout should be covered from interruptions, it would be the first 4-5 hours of sleep.

For many parents, it is impossible to achieve this ideal state in the days immediately after childbirth. If this is your case, you can take heart: When people are severely deprived of sleep — suffering from a significant NREM3 deficiency — their brains sometimes react by raising the duration of brief naps.

If you can take a couple of 30-minute naps throughout the day, you can get enough NREM3 to mitigate much of the sleep deprivation's harmful effects (Farout et al. 2015).

However, having your kid to sleep longer — enjoying at least one, 4-5 hour bout of sleep right at your bedtime — will make things simpler. It will offer you the ability to achieve the least and most significant amount of sleep you need to sustain your well-being. In addition, it may be an essential step for your baby to mature, nighttime sleep patterns.

However, will the feeding of dreams work? Will this contribute to more extended periods of baby sleep? Many parents that have tried it feel it works. Their babies sleep in longer, more centralized bouts as the weeks pass. Although we should, of course, allow it to happen anyway. Young infants grow more unified sleeping patterns at night when everything is going well. Below mentioned are the benefits dream feeding can provide you:

Synchronize Your Baby's Sleep with Your Own Sleep

One aim of a dream feed is to match up with your first period of sleep for your baby's more extended phase. Most babies get a longer period of rest, usually in the first half of the night, waking up only when moms calm down in a good stretch of sleep! If your newborn has one or even two night feeds, using a dream feed will get you a more extended period of rest.

Exception for a kid that eats more than one night: Without a dream feed: the child goes down for sleep at 7:00 pm and starts her long 5-hour period. You go to sleep

Montessori First-time

at 10:00 pm, but at midnight, your infant is getting up for a snack. Only Two hours later, the night is cut short!

With a dream feed: Your baby will go down at 7:00 pm for bedtime. Shortly before you head to bed, you are getting a sleep feed at 10:00 pm. Your baby ends her long 5-hour period and wakes at 3:00 am. You have now reached 5 hours of the uninterrupted night!

For babies that sleep in even longer stretches of 8 or 9 hours, that may also mean that your baby sleeps straight to the morning: without a dream feed: your baby goes to bed around 7:00 pm and starts the long 8-hour cycle. At 10:00 pm, you go to bed, and your baby wakes you up at 3:00 am for a feeding. This early morning wake appears to be right in the center of the deepest sleep of a person! (You say that because it is tough to get up and it is much easier to get back to sleep later.) Fuel a dream: the kid goes to bed at 7 pm. Right before you head to bed, you are performing a vision feed at 10:00 pm. Your baby starts its long 8-hour stretch and makes it until 6:00 am. Now you will all wake up comfortable and ready for the day! You had a good night's sleep!

Tank Up Without the Sleep Alliance

One aim of a dream feeding is to start with night feedings with a decreased probability of developing a sleep relationship by night feed. This guarantees that your baby receives adequate calories, but when you start the dream feed as your baby sleeps, and not as a reaction to a call for action, it becomes less likely to become a sleeping crutch. The abdomen of your infant is tanked up, but it is not correlated with the process of falling asleep as he is still sleeping.

Maintain the Supply

A dream feed may be of special benefit to kids who sleep on their own early on in the night, or to moms who have returned to work. In both situations, the supply of mom's milk can take a drop, but you may sustain or even raise supply without needing to put in another pumping session by withdrawing milk from a dream-feed.

Eliminate the Guesswork

Montessori First-time

You have more power of what your baby eats because you are beginning the feeding process. No longer, go to bed worried over what the night is going to look like.

When does a fantasy feed come true?

The dream feed fits well with younger kids under the age of 6 months who are more prone to need a feeding scientifically. In older babies, the introduction of a dream feed appears to disturb the night. In older infants, whether following their lead or reducing excessive feedings is always more successful.

If you are using the dream feed to further balance the long duration of your baby's sleep with your own, you will want to feed your vision before you go to bed. This appears to work best from 10:00 am to 11:00 pm. If you do a dream feed to safeguard your supply or boost calorie intake, the feeding time is less important.

How do I feed on a dream?

It is pretty easy! If you're breastfeeding, just gently pick up your baby and bring it to the breast. Be sure to keep your stimulation low so that you won't wake your baby up completely.

You can pick up the baby or even prop up your baby right in the crib if you are bottle feeding. Never give a bottle to your baby while she lies down. It can contribute to tooth loss or ear infections (both of which will affect sleep — we don't need that!) When feeding is finished, just bring your baby back in her right sleeping place. There is typically no need to burp because your baby is so happy she is less likely to suck in food when eating. In addition, do not think about adjusting it until the baby's diaper is poopy or dripping.

What if I don't latch my baby on my nipple or the bottle?

The deepest sleep of your infant comes in the first half of the night, and at first, she increasingly is challenging to keep latched on. If your baby does not seem interested at first, you may need to transmit a bit of breastmilk by hand and place your baby's lips on your nipple. With formula and a bottle nipple, you can do the same. The scent and taste would possibly entice her to hold on. If your baby sleeps in the breast or bottle, you can use some tactile stimulation, such as rubbing the side of your baby's cheek or using compressions from the chest to increase your flow.

How can I tell that dream feed works?

Offer your baby over a week to calm down in the dream feed routine first. If you feel like you are getting more sleep, then it works for you! If it sounds off, then do not go for it! If dream feed contributes to a longer run, then it works.

For some babies, being even slightly roused during that deep sleep that occurs during the first part of the night can tangle with their rhythm of sleep. Here are few indications that dream feeds may not be perfect for your baby: your baby often wakes up a short period after the dream feed, and you do not have a good rest at night. Your baby wakes up more frequently than when you began to feed your baby during the dream feed and has a rough time resettling to sleep.

One of the dangers of a dream feed is giving the kid the meal period. Therefore, that means your baby can wake up hungry at that time if you do not do the dream feed. It is a smart thing to think accordingly about how you will wean away from the vision feed. It is like weaning your baby off other night feeds.

For younger babies who still need night feeding, push the dream feed over a few weeks later until it falls after midnight sometime. At this point, if she is hungry, you should let your baby wake naturally. You will also get a more extended period of sleep, and your kid will be able to wean this feed on her own. You should withdraw the dream feeding early for older babies who no longer require a meal so that she becomes less hungry and instead remove it entirely. If your baby seems to be hungry at this time, but you are still ready to drop it, you may need to reduce this feeding volume over time by reducing the length of time you're nursing for or the amount in the bottle. By slowly decreasing the amount you lower the risk, she will wake up with a hungry stomach.

Will I leave my baby swaddled to feed on the dream?

A: Most of the time, yes. Let us swaddle your son. You want to stimulate them only a little you can-only enough to feed them. Unsaddling could well wake them up.

What if my kid is too tired and is not going to eat while feeding on the dream?

Some babies are going to need a bit more excitement than some to get them awake up to eat, just make sure you don't rouse them too soon, or they're going to wake up entirely!

- Run a moist wipe or rag over his face
- Brush or tickle the bottom of his foot or jaw
- Place some milk on his lips

If those do not work, lay the baby back down. If you are still up, you can try again briefly a little later. If it is not functioning, so do not push it. "Never disturb a sleeping infant," as they claim. "You would never want to take the risk of making a cranky kid all night if you unintentionally got them up in mid-sleep. If you aim for a couple of nights without results, give it a few weeks' rest and come back to it.

When are you going to continue dream feeding? Is a vision feed too late to try?

Dream feeds work well in babies aged 3-9 months. They need to be fed regularly while your kid is an infant, as their little tummies will only accommodate too much. When they have achieved age around 3 and 4 months, they can continue traveling longer runs. If your baby still has not been able to sleep through the night after nine months of age, however, a dream feed will probably not help as much. Probably other associations of sleep at this age keep them from sleeping a longer stretch at night.

Once the dream feed is done, should I adjust my baby's diaper?

Just when you sense the need. You will learn better after a couple of nights of attempting a vision stream. Again, the idea is to get your baby stimulated as little as possible. They might be wakened by a diaper change, so avoid it if possible. However, if your infant wakes up an hour or two later due to a wet diaper, you may need to make a quick transition after the dream feed before turning them back down.

Bid farewell to Pacifiers

By implementing the Montessori method, pacifiers should not be used widely or will be phased out in the first year. When a small toddler often uses a pacifier, it should not be a complicated task to transition them out.

Even though the child is young, we can let them know we will make a change. The first move is to continue just sleeping with the pacifier. Once our kid wakes, we should place it out of reach in a box by the bed so our kid (or even the adult) will not be tempted to use it. Many days that our child asks for the pacifier, we should seek to understand why they have the urge to suck to fix the root cause. They may need something fun to do with their hands or a gadget to play with, maybe they are searching for a bond so we can give a cuddle, or maybe they need to settle down or ease their nervous system.

Here are a few suggestions that may help:

• sucking milk through a straw

• blowing bubbles

• hanging firmly on to a book or soft toy

• use a bottle through a straw

• blowing water across a straw to make bubbles

• a vigorous towel rubbing during a wash

• deep-pressure bear hugs

• kneading dough

• gripping bath toys

• a steady, hardback rub

We can then create a move for our kid to get rid of the pacifier at one common option is to offer this to a new baby buddy.

It normally takes the infant a couple of days to learn to fall asleep without it, after which they might require some – only enough – extra help. Be alert that no additional sleeping crutches are applied to the routine.

4.3 Understanding your toddler's brain development

The first few years of your baby are a path of learning when its mind expands; its body gets stronger as it learns to grasp the universe and its position inside it. Each and everything provides a learning point, and it is critical that he is introduced to as many development-potential experiences as possible throughout the early years.

Sensory Awareness

There is an old theory that kids know everything they do. Essentially, the same is claimed by Montessori. When we activate the senses of children in ways that allow them to identify and distinguish between the properties of different items, impulses are transmitted back and forth from the nervous system through the brain. The more that occurs, the better the brain neuropathy get, when the brain experiences substantial input that is necessary for proper functioning. Knowing how to think (assimilating, incorporating, and implementing knowledge) later in life relies on whether or not the brain has been "hardwired" correctly at an early age.

We have already identified how babies from the time of birth communicate with the environment through their senses. Montessori thought that we should expand on that by motivating babies and young children to center their attention on the real environment, investigating small differences in the properties of specified sets of items through increasing their senses – seeing, sound, contact, taste, and smell. Exercising the senses of children will significantly enhance their sensitivity through providing experiences that bring their focus to elements of daily life or by unique sensorial practices.

Brainpower boosting exercises to develop sensory awareness are particularly valuable in the years from birth to six, because this is when the nervous system develops.

Ways You Can Develop Sensory Awareness In Your Child

First, the overwhelming news. Your baby's brain is the one big organ that isn't completely developed before he or she is born; it's only 25 percent of the adult brain capacity. It's experiencing tremendous development in the first three years. His or her interactions in those early years continue to build the roots of the brain. In addition, the terrifying part is-what you do (or do not) as parents in these years will actually mold their brain. In addition, what is the better news? That is not complicated to do!

In daily life, we will do small tasks that will add up overnight and make our babies grow wise, socially well adjusted, and caring people. Many things on the list that come as a total surprise-especially their position in the growth of a child's brain.

React faithfully and lovingly

When listening regularly to the needs of your young kid, you do more than give them your affection. You are literally building a stable basis for their brains to develop. Yet still, we fall victim to misconceptions and uninformed suggestions, in spite of our best intentions.

Letting a child weep does not improve the lungs. It causes unnecessary pain. It does exploit him by not picking up a crying infant. It creates commitment and protection problems. Letting the little girl scream to sleep, not teach her to sleep. It encourages her not to confide in men. Any such early exposure allows the brain to wire. If its milk, warmth, and health needs are not fulfilled, the baby's brain is busy thinking about survival. Where is the time to study, learn, and grow?

Give them the power of your touch

'Because touch, more than any other sense, has such ready access to the brains of young babies, it offers perhaps the best and easiest opportunity to mold their emotional and mental well-being,' says Lise Eliot in What's Going In There – How the Brain and Mind Develops in the First Five Years of Life. Cuddling and hugging the infant as soon as we can is the best way to unlock the magic of touch. Not only in reaction to their cries but proactively as well. Yet there are tasks to perform, and homes to manage. Babywearing will assist with that.

You are holding the baby while you're bringing or 'holding' the infant in a sling or some other attachment on your back. Babywearing is shown to suppress screaming in children, allowing them to stay quiet and healthy overall. How is it going to grow the brain? "How do children do in their spare time if they waste less time moaning and fussing about? They are doing! Sling babies invest the most energy in a calm state of alertness. It may be considered a baby's optimum learning environment." says Dr. Sears. One established way we can give the kid major cognitive benefits is by offering him a regular massage.

Talk Loads, Talk Right

There is solid, irrefutable proof from years of study that is talking to your children or especially (who are under the age of 3) is directly related to their IQ and potential academic achievement. Speaking to your child, a great deal is the simplest and most powerful thing you can ever do for them. Day-to-day tasks and even chores give enough chances to chat.

Breastfeed

'The more kids breastfeed, the better they succeed in adulthood – large report,' says The Guardian, Breastfeed as much as your child needs, for as long as possible. Breastfeeding isn't always convenient, so should you encounter some issue, be sure to seek support. There is a range of community networks that are more than happy to assist, both online and offline. Know that breastfeeding is healthier than not breastfeeding at all, just for a brief period.

Talk aloud

To our children, we all realize the value of literacy. Any key points on reading to your child:

- Beginning reading to your kid is never too early – they may be in the nursery, a fetus, or a 6-month-old.
- Carry reading – do not be discouraged if they are just involved in chewing, tossing, or breaking the journal. It is normal; they are going to learn from it.
- Invest in a range of books – dining room, office, bathroom, fridge, baby bag, and car – and scatter them everywhere.
- Set an example – The more you know that you learn, and the more written content you have in the room, the more motivated you become to learn.
- Above all – equate reading with enjoyment. Never using it as a threat, nor force them to learn.

Let them on the run

Work shows close links between physical exercise and brain growth. Making sure your kid has at least 60 (even more) minutes of unorganized physical activity. Sometimes when a kid is upset or ready to throw a tantrum, it will transform the problem around and keep them going. Get crazy, force them to chase you or chase them, launch pillow battles, see who can leap to the highest, play horse-riding on the cushion, mimic animal motions-how frogs run, how rabbits hop, just go insane to get them to move! It will transfer their brain cells too!

Physical exercise includes tummy time for children and allowing them enough space to know how to turn over and crawl. Stop strapping babies in one place in rockers or prams or car seats, as far as practicable (except while driving).

Offer them novelty

'Studies consistently consider it necessary for intellectual growth to have play materials available. Toddlers with a wide variety of accessible playthings later tend to have stimulated mental growth, reports Kathy Hirch-Pasek and Roberta Michnik Golinkoff at the age of 3 and 4 in the novel 'Einstein Never Used Flashcards.' Luckily, we do not have to smash the bank to purchase a new gadget each. By utilizing household items, we should be imaginative; we should change their toys periodically so that only old toys are gazed at with fresh eyes. We may share mates' items or visit toy libraries.

Engage in Sensory Play

Sensory play involves games that allow children to use touch, scent, taste, visual, and hearing senses. The more you use your senses, the more you know. If you are a new mother, you might feel overwhelmed by all the lovely sensory experiences worthy of interest that some moms manage to set up. Fortunately for you, there are many daily household products and events that offer outstanding sensory play opportunities.

- Pool Fun – Bring them a bowl of water and fun to throw with two inside it. Bring them off to the ocean and love rolling in mud or sand 3. Experience Nutrition-Self-feeding is one of the child's greatest sensory opportunities. Let the kid experience and feel the texture of various foods.
- Closet Attack – Open the closet and take out garments in different materials. Play peekaboo with your woolen jumper, place in a tub your cotton dupatta and feel the silk scarf against his face.
- Hot and cold – Reach them with frost, and then a moist (not steam) teacup to tell them about cold and dry.

Encourage imaginative games, get help with chores

When your baby wants to feed a carrot on Teddy, or when your baby dresses up as a fairy and has a tea party, they're pretending to play. Pretend play helps to improve their vocabulary, language abilities, and social skills. Naturally, most children participate in imaginative play beginning about 12 months, and their play gets more complex as they mature. Often, we can support them along – by taking part in the action, introducing the 'show' for the younger kids, providing them with toys (doctor collection, kitchen set, etc.), taking turns playing with them.

When we get little children to support us with age-appropriate tasks, we encourage them to take part in another form of imaginative play, where they become adults. Using easy, day-to-day exercises to teach new ideas. Children who are not yet 3 do not need to study a classroom-type setting. The daily existence and artifacts provide ample opportunity to teach them simple concepts.

Encourage them to share stories

When a kid tells us a story, it brings all of her imagination into motion. 'The left brain will place things in order, use vocabulary and reasoning, to say a tale which makes sense. The right brain contributes to the body's feelings, raw emotions, and personal experiences, and we can see the whole image and interact with The Whole-Brain Kid, our experience' writes Dr. Daniel Siegel.

Modeling story-telling will build the groundwork for parents. Narrate previous kid incidents and envision potential 'lines.' As soon as they start talking, allow them to share their story, listen closely, address questions that will enable them to speak more. The best way is to spend a few minutes with your child every night passing the day.

Lay the framework for successful music

Listening to Mozart has a little long-lasting impact on the intellect of a boy. The theory was debunked. Yet playing a musical instrument remains linked to knowledge.

We can't teach babies to play an instrument, of course, but we can set the foundations for them to equate music with pleasure. Singing to them, singing rhymes while we sing, motivating them to sing along, will help them see music while enjoyable, and make them content. So maybe as they're a little older, we will expose them to different musical instruments and see what they're really loving playing.

Ensure sure they have the night.

'Sleep is the source of energy which keeps your brain alert and relaxed. Sleep recharges the brain's battery every night and at every nap.' says Good Sleep Patterns founder, Happy Boy, Marc Weissbluth, MD Young Baby Parents usually do their hardest to ensure their children sleep well. Or just lay it off! We can be sure we don't do anything that hampers their sleep unknowingly. Either allow them to have screen time up to 2 hours before bedtime, not providing enough productive daytime playtime, or prioritizing our routines over the sleeping timings of our kids.

Brain Development

From Birth to Age Three: An Overview of Early Brain Growth

First Trimester

In the first several weeks of pregnancy, brain development ends. Many of the brain's developmental features emerge throughout the embryonic stage (approximately the first eight weeks following fertilization); these constructs then begin to expand and mature throughout the fetal era (the rest of gestation).

The first primary process in brain growth is neural tube creation. Approximately two weeks after birth, the neural shield, a sheet of advanced embryo cells, starts to fold gradually over into itself, ultimately creating a tube-shaped framework. The tube closes slowly as the sides of the plate connect; normally, this cycle is accomplished four weeks after conception. The neural tube keeps evolving and finally becoming the brain and spinal cord.

The first neurons and synapses start to form in the spinal cord about seven weeks following conception. These early neuronal contacts enable the fetus to make the first movements, that can be sensed by ultrasound and MRI even if the mother can't feel them in most cases. Such gestures, in effect, provide sensory feedback to the brain that will accelerate its growth. More synchronized motions develop during the next few weeks.

The Second Trimester

Early in the second trimester, gyri and sulci begin to show on the surface of the brain; this cycle is nearly complete by the end of this trimester. The cerebral cortex increases in thickness and sophistication, and the development of synapse starts in this region. During the second trimester, Myelin begins to develop on the axons of individual neurons. This cycle persists through puberty-named myelination. Myelination makes for better information processing: for the brain to reach the same degree of output without myelination, the spinal cord will have to have a circumference of three yards.

The Third Trimester

The early weeks of the third trimester are a transitional time during which the cerebral cortex starts to fulfill specific roles formerly done by the more basic brain stem. Reflexes like fetal breathing, for example, and reactions to external stimuli, are more normal. The prefrontal cortex facilitates early learning that occurs during this time.

Year One

Newborn babies' impressive abilities demonstrate the magnitude of fetal brain growth. Newborns may recognize human images, which they favor to certain artifacts, and also distinguish between signs of joy and sorrow. A baby at birth acknowledges the voice of her parents and may remember the sounds of stories that her parents read to him or her while they were was still in the womb.

Throughout the first year, the brain begins to grow at a staggering pace. The cerebellum multiplies in volume, which seems to be consistent with the accelerated growth of motor skills happening during this time. When the cortex's perceptual fields expand, the formerly poor and restricted sight of the child grows into complete binocular vision.

The strength of recall in a child increases significantly at around three months; this correlates with substantial development in the hippocampus, the limbic system associated with memory processing. In the first year, the language loops in the frontal and temporal lobes are integrated, profoundly affected by the words a child learns. A baby at an English-speaking home can differentiate between the tones of a foreign language for the first few months. She lacks this capacity at the end of the first year: the vocabulary she learns at home has converted the brain to English.

Year Two

The most drastic developments this year include the vocabulary regions of the brain, which are forming more synapses and being increasingly integrated. Such improvements lead to the rapid increase in the language skills of children – also called the eruption in vocabulary – that usually happens during this era. The vocabulary of a infant even quadruples between the first and second birthdays.

There is a significant increase in myelination rate during the second year, which helps the brain conduct more complex tasks. Higher-order cognitive skills are increasing, such as self-awareness: a child is often more conscious of his thoughts and actions. He now wholly understands anytime he sees his image in a mirror that it is his own. Soon he can continue using his name as well as personal pronouns such as "I" and "me." **YEAR THREE**

Synaptic activity in the prefrontal cortex is expected to plateau in the third year, up to 200 percent of its adult point. The region is also continuing to develop and improve networks with other countries. As a consequence, they promote and combine dynamic cognitive skills. For starters, at this point, children are best prepared to understand current occurrences utilizing the context. They do have more exceptional executive ability and a clear perception of cause and effect. The first signals obtained by the brain have a huge impact.

Early brain growth is the foundation of human endurance and adaptability, but these attributes come at an expense. Since interactions have a high potential to impact brain growth during this time, children are especially susceptible to repeated negative influences. On the other side, these early years provide a window of development for parents, families, and communities: successful first encounters have an immense effect on the prospects for accomplishment, growth, and satisfaction for children.

4.4 Montessori Approach to Toilet Training and Feeding Toddlers

Toilet training is the method of training a young child to control the bowel and bladder and to use the bathroom to eliminate it. A child is known to be qualified as a toilet trained until he or she begins heading to the bathroom and is able to change the appropriate clothes to urinate or move the intestine. Toilet training is sometimes called potty training or toilet learning.

Montessori First-tim

When is the child ready for toilet training?

Many parents are uncertain when and how to start toilet training or "potty training." Not all kids may be ready at the same age, and it's crucial to monitor your infant for indicators of preparation, including stopping operation for a couple of seconds or holding his or her diaper.

Watch for indications that your child might be able to start going for the potty instead of using force, such as:

- obey clear directions to recognize and use terms for using the potty
- create the relation between the desire to pee or poop

Your friend claims that by his second birthday, their little boy became diaper-free. On the other hand, your niece refused to perch at the potty till Montessori. What timeline is appropriate for the potty training? Or state it briefly: zero, neither both. Like for most developmental milestones, infants are equipped for one-of-a-kind routines — so having your child determine the tempo where to start potty training is important.

When your kid isn't equipped for potty training, so all the strongest bathroom methods would probably fall flat. And wait before you see the indicators of this surefire: What are the indicators that my child is about to be taught potty?

1. You change fewer damp diapers. Children pee too often before the age of about 20 months that asking them to regulate their bladders is definitely impractical. But an infant who stays dry at a stretch for an hour or two — and occasionally wakes up without wetness — is physically prepared for potty training.

2. The bowel movements of your infant are regular. If he's getting a BM in the morning, between meals, or right in front of the bed, a daily routine can enable you to know when to take out the potty — and therefore improve his odds of performance.

3. He transmits functions throughout the body. Any kids happily declare that a bowel movement is just about to happen ("I'm pooping right now!"). Some express by fewer vocal means — say, by moving back to a corner or creating a defensive grunt. Whatever the warning, once your kid indicates that he is mindful of the workings of his body, he's primed for the potty training.

4. He scoffs at messy diapers. At some stages, most babies go through a (fleeting) period where they are opposed to personal messes — they're bugged with errant crumbs and dirty paws, and yeah, they're ready to remove their soiled nappies as fast as possible. This is a perfect chance to set start the potty-training cycle, as your kid dislikes the stinky diapers as much as you do for the first time.

5. He will perform quick undressing. The potty will not be of any help as nature calls unless your kid can easily yank off his jeans and pull-ups or socks. Likewise, girls should be able to flash their skirts up.

6. He knows lingo in the toilet. Whether you prefer child-friendly jargon such as "poop" and "pee" or formal terminology such as "defecate" and "urinate," your child will be ready for potty training if he understands and can use the words of the family for bathroom functions and any related body parts.

Montessori Parents Toilet Training

What makes Montessori toilet training different is that it follows the child's development, and respects every child. It is slow, and at the speed of the infant. If your child/toddler attends a Montessori school, ask whether they have any childrearing or toilet learning handouts or if they operate any seminars or information sessions on the topic. It is better to read up on the subject wherever possible when your child is still in infancy.

Indirect Toilet Preparations

From birth, practice changing your child's diaper to give plenty of indirect kind of preparation as soon as it is wet (this can sometimes mean as often as every hour). From the beginning, the usage of cloth diapers allows tremendously to gain understanding, as they instinctively feel warm. This positive input makes the infant equate the desire to urinate to the outcome of relaxing her muscles. Thereby toilet training takes place slowly, over time. When the child is going to pull up and stand, let her rise when you are adjusting her and chat about what you are doing, include the child where you can. She will see what is going on and take an interest along that direction. Unless you have not already done so, as your infant begins to rise and walk, shift the diaper to the toilet. This helps them build the right connections between action and location.

The critical time for initiating toilet knowledge is between twelve and eighteen months when to start the toilet. Depending on the child, it will start eventually. Look for signs of readiness:

- Interest in cycles (bib is now going into the hamper, the hamper is going into the basement, into the machine, etc. Child watches with interest and even goes along).
- Baby runs.
- You note an infant is rubbing her / his genitals.
- For other hours during the day, the infant begins experiencing bowel movements.

Often a kid displays neither of these symptoms but gets excited as soon as you start directing her attention to the toilet, and we also suggest starting before 18 months.

Toilet Performance Tools

You could buy 30 pairs of thick underpants to get going. Gerber training pants that come three in a pack for around five bucks are suggested. They are the most absorbent but robust and the least costly. The leg holes must be wide enough for performance, and the underwear loses enough so it can be pulled up and down on the child's part without any additional effort. (Gerber training pants, size two, are suggested for an infant aged between 12 and 18 months. As the child reaches 18 months, or when she's large for her age, size three would be expected.)

Place a slice of rubberized flannel in the back of the car and purchase a couple of sheets for the bunk. Make sure you have plenty of pairs of pull-on pants for your boy because he will need to change sometimes. Include plenty of sheets, and you can rotate them regularly. Pick up delicate rugs.

Find "Nature's Gift" at a pet shop to clean rugs or the floor easily and efficiently, if desired. The item eliminates not only the mark but also the scent, which is suitable for good rugs and can be kept easily on the rug.

Place tiny potty chairs, a range if appropriate, and allow the child to sit on them, encouraging them when they do. Place a potty in each toilet with a small bucket to the left, and a clean underwear basket to the right. Under the three things, a folded towel or bath mat provides a non-slip base, and an image organizes.

The first three points are the most relevant as you continue the toilet, as they have to do with attracting your child's focus to this aspect of our everyday lives: let her see you and other family members seated on the toilet as soon as you can. Bring your kid to the bathroom every half hour or so in the beginning and allow her to stay on it whilst seated on the adult bathroom (as would be normal for just a moment). Doing that makes your kid how to use the toilet by the process, so that is even more than telling your infant, "Do you need to go to the bathroom?" That generally guarantees a "No!" except though they need to go!

It is really necessary that your child will quickly move into dry underwear after wetting it. We want her to be used to feeling dry, and to react to wetness right away. Your kid should wear only her panties from the waist down in the early years, and it's easy to use the potty chair to adjust, so it doesn't take long. Timing is crucial as bowel movements go into the toilets! If you note that your child has a bowel movement every day in the same period, make it a normal activity to go together to the bathroom and sit on the toilets. When your child's pacing is erratic, observe him closely and then send him to the bathroom because he goes in his underpants, and you can help him adjust, see the BM go into the bathroom, and push it downwards.

Start your effort to convince him to relax and hang out on the toilet anytime you know there could be a bowel movement coming his way-you might always read books together and pass the time if it happens. Start attempting to get the kid interested in the dressing and undressing. When the kid starts urinating in her bathroom, remind her that you place the pee in the wider toilet and flush. And work closely to remedy her, taking particular attention to making her learn to properly put her dry panties on. And work closely to remedy her, taking particular attention to making her learn to properly put her dry panties on. It helps to have a potty in whatever space he works in the early days so that he can see it and get to it in time. He can only wear pants that are simple to pull up and down himself, and when appropriate during this point, maybe naked or in underwear from the waist down.

When you commence this point, throw out all the diapers. Your kid needs to be set up to excel and have our trust that he will then easily be able to use the bathroom at any moment. A ton of kids sleeps too hard to get up to use the bathroom before they are older. Depending on your kid, her maturity, and the point you have reached in toileting, there are various ways to do that.

Carry a potty chair with you (to use at your destination) during the early phases of the bathroom training as you push your kid out of the vehicle. Place it in the house bathroom you are visiting, even though it is just a brief stay. It may create the bathroom schedule after entering the house and arrival at destinations.

Bring the kid to public bathrooms sometimes when out and about, when leaving home and returning. We suggest that you make it a routine and claim, "We're just sitting on the toilet for a moment before we head out and come home." (Just allow them to stop for a minute whether they stand up or don't urinate, just disregard it and carry on. Hopefully, they'll want to take advantage of the opportunity.) For special occasions or plane trips, we advise you not to bring your kid back in a slide, but instead to place a Nikki slide cover around her panties. With this diaper cover made of lightweight, durable cotton, you should also test for wetness so that the training time is not disrupted. For some public circumstances, this is a good "freedom net" to you. Always have a couple of jeans and underwear changes in the house, so you can run back to the car for a fast change as soon as your child gets dirty and then start shopping.

Tips To Continue Potty Training Once Your Kid Is Eager For Potty Training Success-

- Wear. All that gets in the way is overalls or tricky buttons. Get used to dressing your infant in the right potty training clothes (pants that pull up and down without any easy-to-hike fiddling or dresses).
- Choose a potty chair on the extreme. Some infants prefer a potty seat to their own, and others prefer a separate one. Decide what suits the little one best. If you purchase a seat connected to the toilet, search for a comfortable match — for weeks, a loose seat will spook a child back into diapers.
- Switch on Pull-ups. Pull-ups are a great intermediate level because they encourage you to start practicing in a not-so-convenient position without fear of an injury. Plus, they slide up like underpants, but they can be torn off instead of pushed to his bottom. The drawback is they sweep away moisture like a cloth, and the wetness that can slow down the cycle won't disturb your child. So turn to reusable training pants as you continue to get any accomplishments.
- Look out for signals. You may see them before your toddler at this age. Note whether the little one is straining or fidgeting, then run to the bathroom for a try. There are occasions that you might want to delay starting toilet training, such as: while traveling after a sibling's conception, transferring from the crib to the bed, that your child is unwell (especially if diarrhea is under consideration)

How long does toilet training take?

It's no easy job to train a child to use the potty. It always takes around 3 and 6 months, but for certain kids, it will take more or less time. The cycle appears to take longer if you proceed too early. So remaining dry at night will take months or even years or learn.

Potty Styles

The two main potty choices are a single, adults-sized potty chair with a bowl that can be drained into the toilet with an adults-sized cover that can be put on top of a toilet seat that can help the kids feel better and not scared to fall in. When you want to do so, have a walking stub so that your child can easily touch the seat and be comfortable when making a bowel motion.

Typically it is safer for boys to train to use the bathroom sitting down first before having to pee standing up. A potty chair could be a safer choice for boys who feel uncomfortable — or nervous — regarding standing on a stool to pee in the toilet. With any toilet in your house, you may want to have a potty or seat training. In emergencies, you may also want to have a potty in the trunk of your vehicle. Make sure to take a potty seat with you while driving long distances and rest every 1-2 hours. Then locating a toilet will take too long.

About Training Pants, effective training pants are a helpful move between diapers and undergarments. Since nighttime control of the kids' bladder and bowel sometimes lags behind their daytime regulation, certain parents enjoy using nighttime training pants. Some want their children to wear trousers for exercise while they're out and about. If the training pants remain dry for a couple of days, children will make the transition to wearing underwear.

But some people assume that disposable training undies may make kids believe it's okay to use them like diapers, slowing down the cycle of toilet-teaching. Ask your doctor if the use of disposable training pants as an intermediate phase will help your boy.

Tips for Toilet Training

- You should educate your little one by talking about the method well when your kid is able to use the potty: using phrases to demonstrate the usage of the bathroom ("pee," "poop," and "potty").
- Teach your child to let you know when a dirty or soiled diaper is in.
- Identify habits ("Are you going to poop?"), so your child can know how to understand the need to vomit and pee.

- Get your child to practice sitting on a potty chair. Your child could sit on it at first, wearing trousers or a diaper. Your child can go naked-bottomed when they're ready.
- If you have now made sure that, your child is ready to start studying how to use the potty, these suggestions will help: set aside some time to focus on potty training.
- Do not have your child sit against his or her will at the toilet.
- Show your child how to sit on the toilet and describe what you are doing (because you are helping your child learn). You may even get your kid sitting on the potty seat and observing as you (or a sibling) are using the bathroom.
- Set up a schedule. You may want to continue, for example, by making your child sit on the toilet after arising with a dry diaper, or 45 minutes to an hour after consuming loads of liquids. Only place your child on the potty a couple of times a day for a few minutes, then let your child get up if he or she desires.
- Make your child stay on the toilet for 15 to 30 minutes between meals to take advantage of the normal inclination of the body to get a bowel movement between feeding (the gastro-colic reflex is called this). Many children do have a time of day where they appear to get a bowel movement.
- If you see obvious indicators of needing to go to the toilet, such as crossed hands, grunting, or squatting, remind your child to sit on the seat.
- Empty a movement of the intestine (poop) from the diaper of your infant into the bathroom and warn your infant that poop is going into the bowl.
- Stop hard to pull off clothing, such as overalls and tops that clip onto the groin. Children doing potty training ought to be allowed to undress.
- Offer little incentives to your kid, such as badges or reading time, if your child goes in the potty. Hold a map to monitor milestones. If your little one appears to understand bathroom use, let him or her pick out some fresh pairs of big-kid panties to wear.
- Ensure that all guardians – including babysitters, mothers, and childcare staff – adopt the same schedule and use the same terms for body parts and bathroom activities. Let us exactly how to do the toilet training and remind us to follow the same methods so that the child would not be upset.

125

All efforts to use the bathroom are celebrated, even though nothing occurs. And note there would be injuries. It is necessary not to discipline children with potty-training or express frustration while wetting or soiling themselves or the room. Tell your dad, instead, that it was an accident, and give your help. Ensure your infant is well on the road to use the potty like a big boy.

Problems with Potty Training

A few kids get to use the potty, then never reflect back. Nonetheless, things happen for everyone. Young children sometimes train in stalls and in spurts. Often they also fail or lack their newly learned skills — such as using the bathroom.

As a mom, when your potty-trained infant has an incident, it's normal to feel disappointed, and even angry. Know that regression is simply, in certain situations, a positive emotional reaction to emotions that your child is also not able to convey. And staying calm and taking action to help your kid get back on track is the best option for managing a potty training setback.

What's the gap between the potty training events and the collapse of potty training?

Potty training mistakes arise as the kid tries to use the bathroom first — after all, it is a learning process. Regression, however, occurs when a previously potty trained kid unexpectedly has accidents and/or tries to go back to wearing diapers. The positive news: In most regression situations, the child will catch up only a couple of days or weeks from where she left off.

Popular sources of potty-training relapse. The trick to getting potty training back on track is coping with the sources of injuries, so be on the alert for specific reasons, which could include: lack of preparedness. If the timing is not correct, even all the strongest methods in toilet training do not avoid setbacks. Some children display signs of preparation for potty training between 20 and 30 months, but others may demonstrate these symptoms earlier or later.

Struggle. Every new scenario, such as a new parent, a new sitter, a new daycare, adjustments in the daily schedule of your child, or a family dispute can be upsetting enough to cause a decline in potty exercise.

Feeling sleepy or slow may prevent your baby from going to the potty in order to use it. Pressure on kin. It is possible that moving a child who is not ready or comfortable in using the bathroom would go backfire. During the potty training cycle, it's essential to be polite, compassionate, motivating, and calming. Letting your child set the tempo, too, is important. Length. Whether your kid is busy playing or engaging in some task, she might not feel the need to go to the potty until it's too late, or she might want to postpone going only because she doesn't want to interrupt what she's doing. Excitation. Just becoming excited may cause an accident for the tots who are fresh to the bathroom — they can fail to go or miss the impulse, culminating in an accident. Can't talk. Your child does not have the capacity to convey any apprehension or insecurity over using the bathroom or the actual pain that it might trigger, so that may lead her to want and escape the potty.

Importance of Potty Training

Because infants do not have the opportunity to educate themselves on how to clean themselves in a hygienic environment, potty training is still something any parent will undertake as part of their child's education, whether they reside in a tribal community or a developing country. The age of potty training varies from birth to preschool, but the benefits are the same, regardless of when you start or where you live.

American Culture specifies that individuals with a diaper will not be removed until early childhood. Therefore, training children to remove in a toilet is important, so that we will not annoy our peers. Even from other parents, this societal pressure comes when a parent considers when using a diaper is no longer acceptable for a child. When the social strain starts, however, it depends largely on what society you live in. In certain societies, potty training begins in infancy, and peers would consider a child in diapers at one or two years of age as socially unacceptable. In the United States, diapers are deemed socially unacceptable only before an infant reaches around four years old.

Self-Esteem and the smallest of children will sense the social burden to use a bathroom. As per pediatrician Jill M. Lekovic in the book "Diaper-Free Before 3," even preschoolers feel the pressure from society to be trained in the potty.

Lekovic claims that potty-trained kindergarteners are more confident than non-potty-trained preschoolers and that being potty-trained for the bathroom allows them "an incredible amount of faith in the environment of preschool socialization." Potty training tends to offer a kid a good self-image and power over her own body.

Good bathroom and potty training have a range of wellbeing advantages. Several research, including the 2002 report "Effects of a questionnaire evaluating the impact of various toilet training approaches on the attainment of bladder regulation" published in the "British Journal of Urology," and research published in the "Journal of Pediatric Urology" in 2009 indicates that subsequent toilet training is correlated with an elevated likelihood of urinary and intestinal disorders, such as urinary tract.

Child Psychology and Toilet Training

Did you know that even back in the 1920s and 1930s, little kids were forced into draconian and abusive measures to provide rigorous toilet training?

According to Gwen Dewar, author of the essay "The Psychology of Toilet Training: What Evidence Tells Us about Timing," in 1935, the U.S. Department of Instruction suggested the usage of soap sticks injection into the rectum at all hours to impose rigid regularity of bowel movement. Others also levied severe penalties on incidents concerning bathroom instruction. Dewar said such brutal practices were widespread shortly after the Second World War, where the scientific profession protested about their harmful impact on infants. Let's take a deeper look into the social effects of potty training to fully grasp this.

Potty Training And Erikson's Psychosocial Development Theory

Erik Erikson, inventor of the eight-step Psychosocial Development Theory, emphasized the significance of effective potty training in the second growth period called Control vs. Guilt and Skepticism. According to Erikson, when an adult grows up, there are many phases of psychosocial growth that need to be commenced successfully. Failure at any point to resolve the war will contribute to psychological distress and social misdemeanors.

He said in his hypothesis that when an infant hits 18 months to 3 years of age, they undergo an emotional conflict for sovereignty. If you have contact with kids, you realize that these kids like to tell "No" a lot and want to determine for themselves what food to consume or what clothes to wear. This is because they feel a sense of "control" over their kin. Through managing stuff themselves, they build a perceptual illusion of sovereignty. With respect to potty training that often remains true. If a child is taught effectively through these years, they will establish a sense of sovereignty that will ultimately lead them to "should" virtue. If the child does not do this, though, it may contribute to a psychiatric breakdown of guilt and doubt. Erikson theorized that failure at this point gives rise to certain negative effects on the psychological and social functioning of a child, particularly the following:

- The child may have low self-esteem.
- The child becomes overly reliant on others.
- They would challenge each other in accomplishing various activities.
- They are likely to grow up with a lot of insecurities.
- Sometimes, they'd condemn their own skills.

It takes us to another matter. How can we claim a kid has had a good potty training?

Successful Vs. Unsuccessful Potty Training

The position of parents, is very important in potty training an infant. Parents will encourage freedom for the child without resulting in a lack of self-esteem for the child. So a delicate balance should be kept in order to be effective in getting our child to learn his toilet routine. How do we continue to do this?

Let the infant demonstrate its readiness to be taught in the bathroom. We can verbalize a need to go to the bathroom or use the toilet. Forcing them to do so even if they do not feel the desire can result in psychological distress. Let your child have enough time in the toilet. Let them learn their routine themselves. Too much interaction and rigid habits will just discourage your boy.

Show not relaxation but gratitude. When your little one has been good, compliment them with stuff like "Great work! "And" You have made it correctly! "Instead of verbalizing gratification such as 'Finally, you did it' or 'Finally, it's over.' Encouraging the kid would make them more comfortable about their self-control and motivate them to do something again, whilst the other will offer the pessimistic notion that you're sick of waiting or that you only want to finish it up. Don't mention anything bad. Any definitions are, "You've never grown," or "You're always getting things wrong." Telling your kid of their failed potty training or making someone know about it can impact their sense of self-worth.

Evite the kid getting scolded for injuries. Your child has yet to learn its own bathroom routine, and accidents can occur. Scolding them will contribute to deterrence. Try rephrasing the sentences as something like, "I hope you should do something different this time" or "I'm sure you'll be able to make this error again."

Tips for managing potty training failures

Picking up pee puddles is especially stressful because you figured you'd already hit this landmark of progress. But have confidence. It's only a process, and your little one gets beyond it. These tips may help:

- Be relaxed. After an incident, your child can get frustrated, so be careful. ("You've had an incident, so that's all right. Tons of kids have incidents; maybe you're going to make it to the potty on time this time.")
- Never scold, threaten, or blame your kid for experiencing a failure.
- Potty Training Ideas for Boys and Girls
- Continue to play Fun Play Baby Playing, Walking, Leaping, and Kicking

Note that the method varies with all ages. Although most children are taught potty by around three years, all children grow at various levels, and some will require more time. So be confident that your child is old enough and shows signs of preparation.

Shooting problems

Montessori First-time

Does your child appear exhausted or stressed out? Worried? Discuss potential reasons for a setback with your kids. ("Are you worried about moving to our new home?" or "Has your new brother been changed at home?") And attempt to help her express her thoughts about what is troubling her. Then, you should provide reassurance to help create confidence. ("It's normal to feel scared of your new daycare, but those feelings are going to go away.") Go back to the starters of potty training. Be clear on when to use the potty and how. Suggest regular breaks in the bathroom at key times, like first thing in the morning, after meals and snacks, before a car ride and before bed, but try not to nag. Try utilizing (or re-activating) a stickered incentidve program.

Boost the likelihood of your child succeeding. Hold the potty in a convenient spot, and dress your kid in easy-to-use, easy-to-go bottoms. Look for training pants. Training pants will make potty training less inconvenient if you're on the early side, and help teach wetness sensitivity with adorable icons that disappear as they get wet. If your kid is in potty training later, you might choose to continue with pull-ups when incidents become uncomfortable (such as while you're away from home), only using regular pants during training sessions at home.

Offer appreciation for every move along the way. Play the "big baby" angle to help inspire your kids. When she effectively uses the potty, emphasis on constructive encouragement, and enthusiastic support. If you have ruled out any potential factors and the regression of your child continues for more than a month, she may just not be able. Under any scenario, offer a little break to the potty training. Only get back on track as soon as your child begins to display indicators of anticipation because discipline is vital to progress.

What to contact the doctor regarding the worsening in potty training or injuries?

Injuries is part of the cycle of potty training, but repeated incidents for an extended time may be a sign that there could be a medical problem that requires care. Test with your pediatrician whether your kid has either of these symptoms: persistent wetness Wetness after laughing A weak urinary stream Frequent urination or defecation Recurrent constipation Blood in the pee or stool Your pediatrician may help diagnose either physical or non-physical complications that your kid might have, as well as offer advice for treatment, behavioral changes.

Feeding Toddlers

For the young, fruits and vegetables make perfect snacks. They are filled with vitamins and nutrients, as well as valuable concentrations of minerals and trace minerals. They do happen to be small in calories, calcium, and fat, both of which are essential components to help the growth and development of your toddler. Fruits and vegetables will star at all meals and are an excellent addition at snack time, so by incorporating them along with other nutritious snack items, you are improving the diet's energy and nutrient content.

Here are a few, fast and simple ideas for baby snacks that include vegetables and fruits.

Fruit With Cheese Frais

As with all dairy products, cheese Frais is an excellent source of muscle and bone density protein. Fromage frais is also filled with B vitamins, required to release electricity. While the tiny pots of fruity cheese frais are always sugar-laden, serving fruit slices alongside simple cheese Frais is an excellent choice for a healthy snack. Fruit, peach, banana, mango, and melon strips all fit just fine for dipping. The smoother quality of cheese Frais renders this dip less sticky than regular yogurt.

Fruit With Cheese Cubes

Cheese is known to be high in calcium and phosphorus, which are both critical for bone growth. Apple bits, grape pieces, raisins, or even celery sticks come perfectly paired for a snack with the milk. Cream cheese pineapple as a coating cream cheese is lower in salt than strong cheeses like Cheddar but also a decent choice for calcium bone building. Top cut mini bagels, crackers, or toasted crumpets containing soft cheese and pineapple slices. Canned pineapple is a much more versatile choice than fresh pineapple, but only make sure that the rings or pieces are well-drained because the juice will get soggy the bread or crackers. For a cold, yummy snack or dessert during warmer weather, pulse light berries that are frozen with a blender, and stir through natural or Greek yogurt. The effect is identical to ice cream even without having all the sugar in it.

Freezing the mashed banana is another good ice cream option; you can also put it in lolly molds. If you don't have time to prepare, choose your hummus with frozen chickpeas, tahini, garlic, and lemon extract than store-bought hummus is always the right choice for your little one. If your tot continues to follow a vegan or vegetarian diet, then hummus adds additional protein, calcium, and iron as well. Naturally, pepper and carrot sticks are good, while cucumber and celery sticks are often ordinary when infants are growing teeth.

So now you know, there's no need for boring infant snacks. You could sustain your little one's diet varied with a range of sweet and tangy options to choose from and will provide them with nutrients they need for growth and development.

4.5 Effective Parenting Methods that actually work & Advice for New Mothers

You've gone through labor, labor, and childbirth, and now you're excited to go home and continue your baby's life. But, once back, you can feel like you have no idea what you are doing. These strategies will make even the most stressed first-time parents feel assured that they can take charge of a child within no time.

Having Aid After the Birth

Remember seeking assistance that may be quite hectic and stressful at this period. Speak to the professionals around you when inside the facility. Many clinics have diet experts or lactation counselors who will help you get breastfeeding or bottle-feeding going. Nurses are also an excellent tool for teaching you how to carry, burp, feed, and look after your infant.

You may choose to employ an infant nurse, postpartum doula, or a conscientious community adolescent to support you for a brief period after conception for in-house assistance. Your doctor or hospital may be able to help you locate in-house support records, and can refer you to home health agencies. Relatives and acquaintances are usually keen to support. Also, if you differ with specific issues, do not doubt their expertise. Yet do not feel bad for putting limits on travelers if you do not feel up to receiving guests or have any issues.

Handling a New Born

If you have not been around newborns for a long time, their fragility can be overwhelming. Here are a few tips you should remember: Wash your hands before touching your infant (or using a hand sanitizer). Newborns do not yet have a good immune response, and they are at risk of being sick. Ensure sure everybody who touches your kid has their hands washed.

Help to the head and neck of your infant. Cradle your back while holding your infant, and keep your head while bringing the infant upright or while lying down your baby. Never shake your baby, in practice, or out of rage. Shaking of the brain will cause damage and even death. Should not do so by tossing if you intend to wake your child — either tickle your baby's foot or softly blow on an ear. Always sure, the infant is safely secured to the backpack, car seat, or stroller. Stop some operation, which may be too rough or bouncy. Note that the infant is not equipped for physical activity, including getting knee-jiggled or tossed into the air.

Bonding

Supportive Bonding, perhaps one of the most pleasurable aspects of childcare, happens in the first hours and days after conception during the critical period when parents create a meaningful link with their baby. Physical closeness can encourage emotional bonding.

For children, attachment leads to their emotional growth, which in other ways, such as physical growth, often influences their progress. Another way to conceive about connecting with your kid is by "falling in love." Children succeed in their life by finding a parent or other person who loves them unconditionally. Start bonding by cradling your infant and stroke him or her softly in various patterns. You and your wife should even take the chance to be "head-to-skin," either eating or cradling, hugging your baby to your own flesh.

Babies may respond to massage, especially premature babies and those with medical problems. Other forms of massage can improve bonding and assist with the growth and development of infants. Many books and videos address the treatment of children-ask the doctor for advice. Be cautious, though — babies are not as heavy as adults are, so gently massage your infant. Babies seem to enjoy expressive noises like talking, babbling, humming, and cooing. Your kid will definitely love to listen to music as well. Some effective methods to enhance the infant's ears are baby rattles and electronic mobiles. Consider humming, reciting poems and nursery rhymes, or speaking aloud as you swing or softly rock your infant in a chair if your little one is fussy. Some babies may be unusually sensitive to touch, light, or sound, and could easily startle and cry, sleep less than expected, or turn away their faces when someone speaks to them or sings to them. Hold noise and light rates low to moderate if this is the case for your infant.

Swaddling

Swaddling, which functions best throughout the first few weeks children, is another calming method that parents will practice the first time. Proper swaddling holds the limbs of a baby tight to the chest, thus allowing any leg mobility. Swaddling not only holds an infant safe but also appears to offer a feeling of protection and warmth to most newborns. Swaddling may also help to limit the reflex of astonishment that can wake a child. Here is how to swaddle a baby: Stretch the receiving sheet, one corner partially folded over.

- Lay the baby face-up on the blanket, over the folded corner with his head.
- Wrap the left corner over the baby's body, and tuck it under the baby's back, under the right arm.
- Take the bottom corner up around the foot of the infant and raise it over the ear, pulling back the cloth as it comes near to the nose. Make a careful note to curl up around the waist too closely. Hips and elbows should be twisted slightly and will turn down. Too tightly wrapping your baby may increase the chance of having hip dysplasia.
- Wrap the correct corner around the infant; tuck it on the left side of the baby's ass, leaving just the neck and head uncovered. Make sure you can move a hand between the blanket and the chest of your baby to ensure that your baby is not bundled too closely, which would make for easier breathing. However, make sure the blanket is not so loose it might become undone.

Babies should not be swaddled after two months. Few babies at this age can turn over while swaddling, which raises their risk of sudden infant death syndrome (SIDS).

Montessori First-time

Everything Regarding Diapering

You will actually know whether you are going to use a cloth or disposable diapers before you carry your baby home with you. Your little one can dirty diapers approximately ten times a day, or about 70 days a week, no matter what you have.

When diapering your baby, be sure that you have all the tools within reach such that you do not have to put your infant on the changing table unattended. You will need: a clean diaper fastener (if disposable presold diapers are used) diaper ointment diaper wipes (or a hot water cup and a clean washcloth or cotton balls) after each bowel movement, or if the diaper is sticky, put your baby on his or her back and remove the messy slip. Using the bath, cotton balls, and washcloth or the towels to clean the genital region of your baby gently. Take very cautiously when changing a boy's diaper, because access to the environment will cause him to urinate. To prevent urinary tract infection (UTI), clean her bottom from front to back while wiping a child. Apply ointment to avoid or treat a rash. Mind also to wash your hands properly following a diaper shift.

A diaper rash can be a problem specific to you. The rash is usually red, which bumpy and should go away with warm water, some diaper cream, and a little time without the diaper over a couple of days. Some rashes develop when the baby's skin becomes responsive, and the dirty or poopy diaper is irritated. Use these strategies to prevent or treat diaper rash: adjust the baby's diaper regularly, preferably during bowel movements as soon as possible. Wash the region carefully with gentle soap and water (wipes may be painful at times), and add a very dense coat of diaper rash or "barrier" cream. Zinc oxide creams are favored because they create a barrier to moisture.

If using cotton diapers, wash them with detergents clean of dyes and fragrances. For a portion of the day, let the kid go un-diapered. This offers the skin an excuse to shine out. Whether the diaper rash lasts for longer than three days or appears to grow worse, call the doctor — it could be related to a prescription-requiring fungal infection.

Bathing Fundamentals

You can give your kid a bubble bath until the umbilical cord falls off and the navel heals fully (1–4 weeks) the circumcision heals (1–2 weeks) The first year's bath is perfect two or three days a week. More regular bathing will dry up on the skin. Before bathing your infant, have these things ready: a nice, warm, gentle washcloth, unscented infant soap, and shampoo a nice brush to relax the baby's scalp towels or blankets to warm Bubble baths and a clean diaper.

At first, you might be nervous to manage a baby but after practicing all these above-mentioned tips, you can establish a routine in a few quick weeks and be nurturing like a pro.

Montessori First-time

Conclusion

Montessori put forward an enticing contrast to her time's restrictive schooling. She took the blueprint from the factory and flipped it over on her back. The philosophy embraced by Montessori was to help rather than threaten, to inspire imagination rather than rote learning, and to inquire for suggestions rather than give responses. She frequently promoted problem solving over rote thinking, initiative over consequences, freedom over control, practical thinking over theoretical learning and preference of satisfying assignments over seeking to appease others. This book is a complete guide for anyone wanting to explore the roots of Montessori, how it emerged, how popular it is today and what exactly are the benefits of sending your child to a Montessori. Each chapter in this book is focused on a different but equally important aspect. The first chapter has not only briefed about who Dr Maria Montessori was but has also covered details of her journey creating the Montessori method. Chapter 1 has also discussed the benefits of Montessori education and compared it with the traditional education today, making it clear how both the methods differ and which one can precisely be more beneficial for your child. The second chapter, as the title says, is focused on making the reader understand the Montessori method in depth. It has discussed the curriculum, lesson plans and a lot of questions that are frequently asked about it. In addition to that, it also has a section for those who confuse Montessori as a constructivist method of learning. Next, the third chapter is a brief chapter yet has everything you need to know when understanding child development from the Montessori method. In addition to that, it has also enlisted the works of different psychologists and how their ideologies matched with Dr. Montessori. The last chapter of the book is itself a complete guide for new parents. It has everything a new parents needs to know, from safe and pain-free methods like Hypnobirthing to baby sleep & feeding techniques for new mothers. It has an interesting part that explains the Montessori approach to toilet training and how it differs from everyday toilet training.

Montessori First-time

References

1. A Brief History of Montessori Education. Retrieved from: https://www.bluffviewmontessori.org/about/a-brief-history-of-montessori-education/

2. Six Fun Ways to Boost Your Toddler's Brain Development. Retrieved from: https://www.todaysparent.com/toddler/toddler-development/fun-ways-to-boost-your-toddlers-language-development/

3. Benefits of Hypnobirthing. Retrieved from: https://www.bmhypnobirthing.com/hypnobirthing

4. Why Choose A Montessori Education. Retrieved from: http://www.webstermontessori.org/why-choose-montessori

5. Independent Sleep and Gentle Parenting. Retrieved from: https://reachformontessori.com/2019/01/07/independent-sleep-and-gentle-parenting-sleep-training/

6. 19 Simple Ways to Boost Brain Power in Infants and Toddlers. Retrieved from: https://www.mylittlemoppet.com/19-simple-ways-to-boost-brain-power-in-infants-and-toddlers/

7. How to Potty Train A Toddler In A Week. Retrieved from: https://www.parenting.com/toddler/potty-training/how-to-potty-train/

8. Dream Feeding a Baby: Its Benefits and Drawbacks. Retrieved from: https://www.momjunction.com/articles/dream-feeding-a-baby_00462342/

9. Learning In the Baby for Preschool Years. Retrieved from: https://raisingchildren.net.au/babies/play-learning/learning-ideas/learning-baby-to-preschool

10. Constructivism and the Montessori Educational Method. Retrieved from: https://www.slideshare.net/tcovert/constructivism-and-the-montessori-educational-method

CPSIA information can be obtained
at www.ICGtesting.com
Printed in the USA
LVHW060115270121
677611LV00006B/392

9 781801 586030